Reviews from Educational Professionals

"As a teacher, I found the content to be highly practical for in-class use. It's nice to have one place to find detailed information on specific apps. The science apps were just what I needed to teach and to allow my students to explore science in a way that has been limited previously. I endorse this book highly and feel all teachers should have this as a critical reference guide in an app crazy world. Busy classroom teachers have so many demands on them today! Keeping up with technology gets pushed down on the list of to-dos. This book provides valuable information for all levels of technology expertise." —**Eric McCullough**, instructor at Columbia State Community College, Murfreesboro, Tennessee, M.Ed. in instructional technology

"I agree wholeheartedly with Carrie Thornthwaite that this trend of cutting art and music in our schools is tragic. Fortunately, I am at a school that holds these areas to a high standard. I am constantly introducing my students to various artists, trying to instill an appreciation for the arts. It is impossible to teach this without visuals. There are no museums in our town that I could even transport the seven-hundred-plus students I see per week. The museum apps are amazing! I could take them through some of my favorites in Europe, Egypt, and even here in the United States through my iPad and projector, and Thornthwaite provides instruction that anyone could follow. These apps are the only feasible way to bring the art to my classroom, and this book makes it so easy!" —**Andrea Myers**, art teacher, Medina Middle School, Medina, Tennessee

"This book is tremendous and the chapter on science apps is awesome! Those apps range from leaf identification, physics, chemistry, to weather and biology. Descriptions offer great detail, even down to explaining look and function of the different buttons in the app. Forty-six apps are listed with some allowing you to zoom out and see the solar system or zoom in to see the organelles of the cell. Some apps have built-in flashcards, teaching videos, picture taking capabilities, quizzing features, and even a listening and reading option to reach many types of learners. The apps featured in the chapter would thrill even Einstein." —**Adam Taylor**, science and Chinese teacher, Metro Nashville Schools, Tennessee, and coordinator of TeachMeet Nashville Technology Conferences

"As more and more schools integrate iPads into their classroom learning environments, books such as Dr. Thornthwaite's will be necessary to help guide teachers and administrators toward best practice ideas. This particular book covers several subject areas often neglected in school technology materials, which makes it a unique resource for educators in those areas. Music educators will find concise, easy-to-understand descriptions of apps appropriate for students in grades 3–12. Personally, I find it difficult to decide on which app to purchase when so many appear to be good, but thanks to Dr. Thornthwaite, now I know which ones I need to buy next! I also appreciate the author including websites, when available, so that educators can further investigate an app without having to open a search engine and spend lots of time trying to find the correct site." —**Katie Frazier**, music teacher for Middle Tennessee Christian School, Murfreesboro, Tennessee

The Deuce and a Half iPad

Also by the Author

Not a Toy, but a Tool:
An Educator's Guide for Understanding and Using iPads

The Deuce and a Half iPad

An Educator's Guide for Bringing Discovery, Engagement, Understanding, and Creativity into Education

Carrie Thornthwaite

ROWMAN & LITTLEFIELD
Lanham • Boulder • New York • London

Published by Rowman & Littlefield
4501 Forbes Boulevard, Suite 200, Lanham, Maryland 20706
www.rowman.com

16 Carlisle Street, London W1D 3 BT, United Kingdom

British Library Cataloguing in Publication Information Available

Library of Congress Cataloging-in-Publication Data

Thornthwaite, Carrie.
    The deuce and a half iPad : an educator's guide for bringing discovery, engagement, understanding, and creativity into education / Carrie Thornthwaite.
        pages cm
    Includes bibliographical references and index.
    ISBN 978-1-4758-0936-7 (cloth : alk. paper) — ISBN 978-1-4758-0937-4 (pbk. : alk. paper) — ISBN 978-1-4758-0938-1 (electronic) 1. Computer-assisted instruction. 2. iPad (Computer) 3. Tablet computers. I. Title.
    LB1028.5.T518 2014
    371.33'4—dc23
                                                                          2014001739

Printed in the United States of America

Contents

Preface

iPads are powerful tools for stimulating:

1. Discovery
2. Engagement
3. Understanding
4. Creativity
5. Enhanced learning environment

I have come to that conclusion after three years of working with iPads in a variety of academic settings. I quickly developed a passion for using iPads in the classroom and want to share that passion.

Most of the chapters in this book were written prior to having a title for the book and prior to writing the first chapter. As I struggled with a title, I knew that I wanted to emphasize the five words mentioned in the first paragraph. I wrote down the five letters that began each of those words and suddenly the word "DEUCE" jumped out at me. With a little more research, the title of the book quickly became obvious to me. Further explanations are covered in chapter 1.

This book is part of a two-book set. The companion book is titled *Not a Toy, but a Tool*. Both books have been written so that principals, media specialists, teachers, and parents can understand the tremendous value provided by iPads in the field of education. The information in both books covers all subject areas and grade levels, in order to share the reasons for my convictions and to recommend a large collection of apps that are perfect for enhancing teaching and learning in today's classrooms. In addition, both books provide information for users of other tablets.

While I have been excited to share all the information in both books of the two-book set, I was particularly thrilled to cover each of the subjects in this book. Over the years, for a variety of reasons, I have developed a deep vested interest in each of the topics that are covered in the separate chapters of this book. Chapter 2 covers mathematics. I was a former geometry teacher and still miss being able to play with numbers and to share hands-on activities with my students.

Chapter 3 covers science. My major in college was physics; while teaching at the high school level, I always loved sharing my passion for physics. My primary reason for choosing that major was that the labs fascinated me. At my high school position, I once received a grant for $20,000 worth of equipment. I was able to do multiple labs with my students every week.

Chapter 4 covers art and music. The introduction to that chapter shares my passion for those areas. I am not talented in either area, but I have a deep appreciation for both areas of study. Chapter 5 covers health and physical education. In my teenage years, I was an All-American swimmer, competing at both national and international competitions. For a few years, I worked as an age-group coach. As a result, I am passionate about the value of being involved in sports and of staying healthy at all ages.

My love for English Language Learner (ELL) students began during my years of high school teaching. In the mid-1980s, the high school where I taught was designated as one of two high schools in the city to provide programs for the ELL students. I grew to respect these students who often had to overcome great hardships just to earn entry into this country. Once here, they tended to greatly value the education that was being provided to them, as often in their homelands they had not been allowed to receive any formal education.

The final chapter covers the areas of special education. My passion for those areas stem from the fact that I have had family members who received services, in several areas of special education. The iPad has much to offer all these topics and it is my pleasure to be able to share the collection of over 220 apps covered in this book.

Acknowledgments

To my guides . . .

In my role as teacher and professor, I have always tried to hold as much as possible to the adage of being a "guide on the side," rather than the uninspiring lecturer acting as a "sage on the stage." As I reflect over the year and more that was needed to assimilate the information contained in the book, I realize that the final product would not have been possible without many guides on the side who gently helped to move me through the process of publication. My gratitude to each of these folks cannot be overstated.

Above all, my deepest gratitude goes to my dear friend, Melanie Crotty, who served for many years as the reference librarian at the Burlington County Library in New Jersey. Melanie read every page of the prepublication manuscript, editing each chapter with expertise and diligence. In addition, we discussed together many ways to improve the chapters.

Immense gratitude should also be expressed to Phillip Brackett who serves as the technology specialist at Lipscomb University's Information Technology Center. Phillip read and edited the first few chapters; additionally, he served as my technical expert on iPads.

My friend Emily Wilson-Orzechowski read the chapter on apps for the English classroom. She spent considerable time editing and adding suggestions. As a physics major, writing was never my first love. Emily, however, is the former writing center coordinator at Hartwick College in Oneonta, NY. Her expertise was immensely helpful; the notes she provided assisted me with my writing throughout the remainder of the book.

My colleague Nina Morel, co-director of Lipscomb's College of Education Master Program, was tremendously helpful in guiding me through the first steps toward publication. Nina read and edited the first chapter of the first book of this two-book set. As a published author, her advice gave me considerable insight into the struggles that I might face.

Jesse Savage, a principal at Lipscomb Academy was extremely kind in providing advice and time. Through early discussions, Jesse helped me understand the difficulties inherent with using shared iPads. After using carts of iPads for several years, Lipscomb Academy has now begun a 1-to-1 iPad initiative, thanks to the tremendous work of Mr. Savage. He allowed me to attend professional development sessions that he taught for his teachers concerning classroom uses of the iPad.

Having considerable experience in both secondary and postsecondary education, I had clear ideas of how iPads could enhance instruction in those classrooms. However, originally I had some difficulty envisioning the use of the iPad in elementary classrooms. Then I met Timothy Carey, the Media Arts teachers for K–4 students at Henry C. Maxwell Elementary in Antioch, TN. I was able to observe him using the iPad as an art-making tool with apps like Brushes, Puppet Pals HD, and Faces iMake. Even with kindergarten students, the iPads served at great tools. I appreciate Mr. Carey's willingness to let me observe his classes and to also discuss with him the insights he had on how to successfully use iPads with very young children.

Finally, thanks to others who helped me more indirectly, especially on some difficult days when events seemed to distract from my writing. Those include my husband, my colleague Carole, my church family, and other family members.

Finally, I'd like to dedicate this book to my precious newborn grandson, Axel Leonard Miller, who, with the guidance from his older brother, will undoubtedly catch on quickly to the use of iPads.

Introduction

This book is part of two-book set that delves into the tremendous value that iPads can provide to educators. This book focuses primarily on iPads for two reasons: (1) Apps tend to hit the iPad market first; some may be adapted for other tablets later. (2) The quantity of educational apps on iPad far exceeds the number available on other tablets. However, in recognition that some educators and students may have access to other devices, apps also available on Android are noted in the app's description. Tablet owners can check later to see if additional apps become available on their devices.

Both books of this set start with a chapter based on research; all subsequent chapters focus on apps appropriate for specific subject areas. Chapter 1 of this book starts by sharing research that relates to how iPads are excellent tools for stimulating (1) *discovery*, (2) *engagement*, (3) *understanding*, (4) *creativity*, and (5) an *enhanced* learning environment. Chapter 1 explains how each of those terms led to naming this book the *Deuce and a Half iPad*.

The first book of this two-book set is titled *Not a Toy, but a Tool: An Educator's Guide for Understanding and Using iPads*. After an initial chapter based on research, that book focuses on two areas: (1) apps that have value for all educators and (2) apps that have specific value for teachers of the humanities. After the research chapter in this book, the focus is on six different areas:

- Mathematics
- Science

- Art and music
- Health and physical education
- English language learning
- Special education

Throughout the book, two criteria were used for selecting apps: high quality and low cost. Each app mentioned in this book has gained high ratings, usually from multiple sources, including iTunes and often one other source. Apps that were free or $1.99 or less were originally selected. In a couple of cases, a $2.99 app has been listed because the quality of the app warrants the additional expense.

Within the various sections and also at the end of most chapters, websites are listed that provide additional information. Also, throughout each of the chapters, listings are included for additional highly rated apps. The listings are specific to subject areas and grade levels. Although highly rated, some of those apps cost more than the $1.99 limit. The cost is usually why they are not fully described in the chapter. The reader can make the decision whether the value warrants the additional cost.

Finally, in some chapters, there are lists of apps that are described in other areas of the two-book set. For example, PrepZilla is an app that is discussed fully in chapter 2 on mathematics. However, the app also covers several science subjects: advanced placement (AP) chemistry, AP physics, AP environmental science, and Regents Exam: biology. So the app is also listed near the end of chapter 3, which covers science.

Descriptions of apps are primarily overviews. With the limited space, descriptions could not possibly include every bell and whistle within each app. However, the descriptions provide enough information so that readers will be able to make informed decisions concerning the selection of particular apps from an immense pool.

The instructions in this book also provide readers with an understanding of the key features. In addition, attention is drawn to nearly hidden links within particular apps that open up entirely new areas. Of course, with new updates, even more features may become available, so readers are encouraged to pay attention to updates as they become available.

Another question may arise concerning the durability of the apps covered in these chapters. There is, in fact, a steady flow of apps that do not enjoy a very long survival, although those are generally *not* the highly rated apps. Compared with the more than 900,000 apps currently available, there may be as many 400,000 inactive apps that can no longer be downloaded. However, those apps are nearly always the ones with low ratings; most likely they were dropped because they could not find a sufficient market amid the immense collection of apps.

Two other change scenarios are more likely: (1) an occasional increase in price and (2) the appearance of powerful, newly designed apps that deserve recognition. The fear of price increases is also exaggerated. In fact, while increases do occur, recent trends actually show an increase in the percentage of free apps. A stellar new app that might trump all previous apps in a particular subject area may indeed appear.

A wiki has been created to alert readers to dropped apps, increases in prices, and the appearance of new apps. The wiki will be updated regularly to share (1) the status of all apps covered in this book and (2) the appearance of new apps that show promise for specific areas. After the introductory homepage, the wiki pages are sorted by subject area. A discussion area at the bottom of each subject-area page allows members to comment on existing apps and to add comments about newly discovered apps.

Finally, readers should be aware that some of the websites listed throughout the book may not be available as months pass. Those websites are only included as additional resources or references. If a website disappears that had important instructive information, a note will be made on the wiki and an alternate site will be suggested.

The wiki is private, but readers can request to be a member of this Wikispaces wiki by sending an e-mail to the author. In the message, please include specifically where the text was purchased. Any comments about the book will also be appreciated. Please e-mail carrie.thornthwaite@lipscomb.edu.

Private wiki: iPads for Tools, not Toys: ipad4atoolnottoy.wikispaces.com

More Information on Recent Trends with Apps

- Available apps, 2013: en.wikipedia.org/wiki/App_Store_(iOS)
- 2012 Statistics: 148apps.biz/app-store-metrics/

———⟨⟨⟩⟩———

CHAPTER ONE

The Deuce and a Half iPad

An Educator's Guide for Allowing Discovery, Engagement, Understanding, and Creativity to Enhance the Learning Experience

The title to this book undoubtedly brings on many confused looks. Even the most tech-savvy educators have not heard of the *deuce and a half iPad*. In fact, even the sales reps for Apple would not be familiar with such an iPad. However, this author maintains that *every* iPad is a deuce and a half.

Those with military experience likely know that a *deuce and a half* is the name awarded to the 2-1/2-ton supply truck that the military has used to haul heavy equipment and soldiers to remote areas of combat. The "heavy equipment" for the deuce and a half iPad is the collection of valuable apps that can help a student make great strides toward true understanding. However, using the word *deuce* symbolizes more than just the fact that the iPad can carry an extensive assortment of intriguing and engaging apps.

The five-letter word *DEUCE* is being used in this book as an acronym for the following five terms, each of which has a significant role in augmenting the effectiveness of iPads:

- Discovery learning
- Engaging students
- Understanding more fully
- Creativity encouraged for students and teachers alike
- Enhancement of the learning experience

Figure 1.1. Military Deuce and a Half Truck.
From Wikimedia Commons, commons.wikimedia.org/wiki/File:Deuce_and_a_half_truck.gif.

Discovery Learning with the iPad

Discovery learning is a method that allows students to explore and learn on their own, rather than being spoon-fed information or having to memorize endless streams of facts. In essence, with discovery learning, a student is not given the answer to questions, nor are detailed explanations about the topic provided. Instead, the teacher asks the questions; each student then is empowered to *discover* the answers.

As mentioned in the companion to this book, Mark Van Doren (1944) writes, "The art of teaching is the art of assisting discovery." Serving as the proverbial "guide on the side," the teacher provides the class with materials that allow each student to work toward the discovery of those correct answers. Research shows over and over that students retain information when they are involved with their own learning, rather then just being a receptacle of information.

Science and mathematics are the two subjects that most frequently raise the banner for discovery learning. For example, a teacher might give a class an assortment of circular objects, such as tops of jars, coins, tops of trashcans, or even the circle in the center of the gym floor. Then students discover the value of pi by measuring both the distance around and across those circles. As they see that the ratio comes out nearly the same, no matter how large or how small the object, suddenly pi has more meaning and is no longer just that intimidating concept.

Chapter 3 of this book opens with the following quote from Isaac Asimov: "The most exciting phrase to hear in science, the one that heralds new discoveries, is not 'Eureka!' (I found it!), but 'That's funny'" (Wainer & Lysen, 2009). "That's funny" must have been exactly what French scientist Henri Becquerel said when he opened a drawer where he kept two items, a piece of uranium and photographic film that had been wrapped with light-proof paper. Imagine his surprise when he unwrapped the film and discovered that it was exposed, despite all the protection from light. That "funny" moment lead to the discovery of radiation.

Students need to feel those moments of surprise, when they initially think that something is funny. When students measure various circular objects, as described earlier, some students initially think that it is "funny" that the ratio is constant, no matter how large or how small the circle. Often a student may erroneously assume that a larger circle will have a larger ratio.

Following are three sample questions a teacher might ask students to foster that sense of discover through the use of specified iPad apps:

1. Math, chapter 2: The teacher says, "One can represent 1/4 of a circle, by shading a fourth of a full circle. Is it possible to draw a representation of an improper fraction? Give several examples." Then students use the "Manipulative" section of "Introduction to Fractions" with the *Fractions* app.
2. Science, chapter 3: A teacher queries, "Is there one exact speed needed for a projected object to obtain orbit around the earth? If so, what is that speed?" Then the students use the "Firing Newton's Orbital Cannon" section of the *Exploriments* app.
3. Art, chapter 4: The teacher challenges the students by asking, "If I only give you the colors red, yellow, and blue, would it be possible to color the leaves of a tree green? If so, how?" Students can use the *Color Mixer* app to see the color green magically appear.

As with any discovery learning activity, a student should not just be given an iPad with the hope that discoveries will be made. Teachers must first have a clear objective in mind. Then, with a carefully selected app, a student can indeed realize the discovery and achieve a higher level of understanding.

Engaging Students

The second letter of *DEUCE* refers to "engaging students." Every teacher strives for student engagement. Principals always use student engagement as one of the key criteria for judging a teacher's effectiveness. Innumerable research papers and published articles provide overwhelming evidence that students are engaged when using the iPad as a tool for learning. Below is a small sample of citations that give reference to the engagement provided with iPads:

- "The iPad engages students in ways that no piece of school or classroom technology has ever done." (Faas, 2012)
- iPads provided "increased engagement and frequency of access compared to students using a laptop." (Shepherd & Reeves, 2011)
- "Students' interaction with the device was more personal. You could tell students were more engaged." (Bonnington, 2012)
- "In a survey of some of our teachers who have classroom sets of iPads, 80 percent of teachers said iPads engage students better than desktop or laptop computers. . . . 100 percent of teachers describe students as very engaged when using iPads." (Putnam City Schools, 2013)

Of course, a student would be engaged if a teacher simply let the student play with *Angry Birds*, but these citations refer to an engagement based on educational experiences. Teachers always need to have a clear objective, a carefully selected app, and a thoughtfully designed lesson plan so that the students are engaged in purposeful, educational activities. Several websites already exist that provide teachers with activities, objectives, and lesson plans designed to engage students with a variety of topics. Following are a few sites that provide specific ideas for iPad lessons:

1. *iPad Lesson Ideas* (RM Education)—The lessons here cover ten subjects for middle and high school classes: www.rm.com/_RMVirtual/Media/Downloads/ipad_lessonideas.pdf
2. A twelve-page booklet with subject specific ideas provided through *FlipSnack*: www.flipsnack.com/5C66BE58B7A/d9dfcaf224c60a756003754ec7q45498
3. Listing of twenty-two classroom objectives: edtechteacher.org/index.php/teaching-technology/mobile-technology-apps/ipad-as
4. Four sample lessons: sites.google.com/site/ipadined/sample-lessons

5. *Understanding by Design Lesson Plan* (Mathematics): techmeetsed
   .com/2013/06/16/understanding-by-design-lesson-plan/

Understanding More Fully

Engagement is a goal that, with an iPad, can be achieved by any teacher. However, engagement without promoting understanding represents a futile activity. *Understanding* is represented by the third letter of the acronym *DEUCE*, and arguably represents the most critical component for successfully incorporating the iPad as a valued tool for learning. Understanding is key not only for education, but also in business and marketing. In a training session in London, one speaker made the point that "without understanding, marketing is inappropriate and ineffective" (Brandweiner, 2013).

Every activity undertaken with an iPad should lead the student to an increased level of understanding. Without achieving that goal, teachers waste the valuable resource that iPads provide. Following are just a few citations concerning the relationship between iPad usage and understanding. Each of the five links serves as a valuable reference for additional apps as several of the apps are not fully described in either this book or the companion book, *Not a Toy, but a Tool*:

- High school physics with *iBlackbody* app by Georgia Tech, $0.99—"Making Physics Interactive: New iPad Application Helps Students *Understand* How Conditions Affect Blackbody Radiation": www.gtri.gatech .edu/casestudy/new-GTRI-ipad-application-iBlackbody
- High school math with *ShowMe Interactive Whiteboard* app by Learnbat, Inc., Free—"Student Understanding with the 'Show Me' iPad app": new-to-teaching.blogspot.com/2013/04/learning-about-student -understanding.html
- Middle school math with *Animator* app by JBrown, Free or $0.99—"Animator Free Apps Helps Students Understand Exponents": www.mathy cathy.com/blog/2012/11/animator-free-app-helps-students-understand -exponents/
- Elementary math with *Move the Turtle. Programming for Kids* app by Nest is Great, $2.99—The app is "helpful in understanding of more complex math (algebra, angles, measurement, two-dimensional geometry) and lends itself to connections being made across multiple disciplines": www.ipadcurriculum.com/

- Elementary classes with nine different apps for a variety of subjects—"K–5 iPad Apps for Understanding": www.edutopia.org/blog/ipad-apps -elementary-blooms-taxomony-understanding-diane-darrow

Creativity Encouraged for Students and Teachers Alike

The fourth letter in the acronym *DEUCE* represents *creativity*; the iPad stimulates creativity for students and teachers alike. Encouraging creativity is an issue of paramount importance. Albert Einstein summarized this thought well by stating, "It is the supreme art of the teacher to awaken joy in creative expression and knowledge" (Einstein, n.d.). In other words, teachers should always exude a joy of teaching and learning by *creatively* adapting lessons so that students can understand and acquire new knowledge.

Merely providing students with worksheets exemplifies the exact opposite of a creative lesson. Sadly, far too many teachers, especially at the high school level, merely lecture for 20 minutes and then hand out worksheets for the students to finish by the end of the class. In many such cases, the class is always as quiet as a graveyard. The teacher may pride himself or herself in having excellent classroom management skills, but sadly true learning is not part of the picture.

One summer, a teacher from a nearby school signed up for a workshop at Lipscomb University, in which, due to a large grant, a significant amount of equipment was to be given to each participant. This teacher was well known as someone who taught by lecture and worksheets. He would leave his door open, possibly so that everyone would marvel at his classroom management skills.

At this summer workshop, creative teaching strategies were shared with the participants that would allow students to understand and enjoy mathematics. Most teachers were thrilled to receive the equipment and also to learn about so many new, creative ways of teaching important mathematical concepts. Sadly, the teacher dropped out on the first day. He was furious when he heard that the grant required that he be observed during the fall using the equipment and at least one of the new strategies.

As the teacher stormed out of the workshop, he exclaimed, "No one's going to tell me how I should teach my students!" That teacher had been routinely killing any semblance of creativity that might have still been within his students. And, unfortunately, he was going to continue to do so. And yet, creativity has always been an important part of mathematical and scientific discoveries.

At a 2006 TED conference, Sir Ken Robinson asked, "Do Schools Kill Creativity?" (TEDxTalks, 2007). After honest reflection, most should agree that schools do tend to stifle creativity. The effort to do so may be unintentional, but it does happen. With this country's obsession with standards and testing, teachers are forced to teach massive amounts of information in as short a time as possible. Direct instruction is indeed the quickest, albeit the least effective strategy. Students spend twelve or more years in our schools, experiencing very little variety in teaching methods.

Sadly, it only takes half-a-dozen years to stifle a child's innate spontaneous creativity. Ironically, students then leave the school environment and enter the workforce, only to discover that creativity is tremendously valued and widely rewarded in business environments. An article posted on *Bloomberg Businessweek* (2010) reported, "According to a new survey of 1,500 chief executives conducted by IBM's Institute for Business Value (IBM), CEOs identify 'creativity' as the most important leadership competency for the successful enterprise of the future."

The organization Partnership for 21st Century Skills (2013) is "a national organization that advocates for 21st century readiness for every student." This organization recognizes the importance of creativity by including it as part of its espoused mission to "provide tools and resources to help the US education system keep up by fusing the 3Rs and 4Cs (Critical thinking and problem solving, Communication, Collaboration, and Creativity and innovation)."

In *Checking For Understanding*, Fisher and Frey explain, "The opportunity to apply learning to a novel situation hastens the transfer of learning" (2007, p. 72). The iPad can undoubtedly provide a student with an opportunity to experience "a novel situation." By their very nature, iPads bring creativity into lessons and thus promote learning. Developing the iPad itself required innovation and creativity. The vast majority of apps are innately creative in the instruction of topics.

Following are just four Internet sources that support the capability of iPads to promote student creativity:

- Elgan, M. (2010, April 17). "Why the iPad is a creativity machine." *Computerworld*. Retrieved from www.computerworld.com/s/article/9175687/Why_the_iPad_is_a_creativity_machine
- *iPadCreative* is a blog about using *Brushes* app in art class: www.ipadcreative.com/blog/tag/brushes. More information on this app is available in chapter 4.

- Wilson, J. L. (2013, Oct. 25, Creativity Section, p. 6). "The 100 Best iPad Apps—Creativity Apps." Retrieved from www.pcmag.com/article2/ 0,2817,2362577,00.asp. Eleven Creativity apps are discussed on this one page of a much larger article. Ten of those Creativity apps are very high quality, although expensive. However, *Skitch* for iPad is free and is discussed more fully in chapter 3 of the companion book of this set.
- Klowsowski, T. (2012, April 12). "Your iPad: The creative tool you never knew you needed." *Lifehacker.com*. Retrieved from lifehacker. com/5901341/your-ipad-the-creative-tool-you-never-knew-you-needed. This review focuses on drawing, writing, and music apps.

Obviously subjects such as art and music lend themselves more easily to creativity. Two of these articles are specific to those subjects. This book covers those topics, but it also covers mathematics, science, and health and physical education (PE), special education, and English Language Learner (ELL) students. All subjects should encourage student creativity.

Concerning mathematics, the National Association of Gifted Children (2009) writes, "Allowing creativity back into our classrooms is essential to rekindle an interest in mathematics." In an inspiring TED talk titled "Math Class Needs a Makeover" (2010), Dan Meyer advocated that all students should be encouraged to solve mathematics and science problems in creative ways.

The following list is just a sampling of apps that allow creativity in math classes. The first four are discussed or at least mentioned in chapter 2 of this book:

- *Mathmateer*, Free by Dan Russell-Pinson: Students can design and launch their own rocket, obviously encouraging creativity. The class can discuss the most effective rocket design. A great deal of practice with basic arithmetic is also incorporated.
- *Fractions* by Brainingcamp, $0.99: This app is also described in chapter 3. It was designed to share creative ways to teach about fractions. Fractions can often be intimidating, but this app makes it fun, so that students can understand the effects of increasing or decreasing either the numerator or denominator of a fraction.
- *Chicken Coop Fractions Game* by Lumpty Learning, Free: This app is mentioned in chapter 2, although not fully covered. Most students dread exercises that require converting fractions to decimals. Yet the creative approach taken by this apps thrills students.
- *Geoboard* by The Math Learning Center, Free: Many math teachers have Geoboards, but this allows for two boards without the mess of flying rubber bands.

- *Logic Puzzles HD* by PunkStar Studios, $2.99: This app is not covered in this book due to the cost, but it does encourage creativity, logic, and problem solving.

Creativity and *science* are inseparable. In her online article titled "How Creativity Powers Science," Jennifer Cutraro (2013) quotes cell biologist Robert DeHaan, who shares, "Creativity is a new idea that has value in solving a problem, or an object that is new or useful." All major scientific discoveries required creative thinking, especially when the new discovery overturns previous thinking.

Often highly educated folks are uncomfortable with creativity. Einstein proposed his theory of relativity as a creative way of looking at the universe. Many of his peers baulked at Einstein's ideas. Thus he was never awarded a Nobel Prize for his theory of relativity, but rather for his discovery of the photoelectric effect. The photoelectric effect was much more easily demonstrated, showing that light can generate electricity. The Nobel committee refused to recognize the much more creative theory, despite the fact that astronomers validated the theory during the 1919 solar eclipse.

In another example of creativity-fueled science, sailors had puzzled for years why the masts of approaching ships were viewable before the base of the boat. Scientists in several cultures began to suggest that the world was round. Again, many were afraid to think creatively. Poor Galileo was condemned to house arrest for the last nine years of his life due to his courage in looking at the world differently and standing alone to champion heliocentrism.

Over and over, creativity leads to discovery. Science teachers need to encourage creativity. Some scientists today may be on the verge of disproving one of the "facts" included in our current science textbooks. Teachers must not be afraid to think creatively and to accept creative thinking from students. Creativity is a basic part of scientific thinking.

Most apps in chapter 3 include some aspects of creativity. For example, the *Science 360* app for iPad includes a large collection of creative videos that show scientific theories playing out in real-world situations. The *Rockets* app allows a student to "work" for NASA building and designing a rocket. With the *Power of Minus Ten* app, students can view details of the human hand, from the surface skin level to the atomic level. Students are fascinated with the *Exploriments* app, which offers several experiments that all relate to gravity.

Creativity is equally important in the sports arena. Those hard and fast rules are actually not so rigid. Creative coaches or athletes may suggest better or safer ways to play the game. For example, in the 1930s, some athletes

began to enter breaststroke events and swim them like the current-day butterfly. At the time, the rules for breaststroke simply stated that the arms and
legs must move simultaneously. These creative swimmers had not broken the
rules, but they obviously far outswam the competition. The new stroke was
not officially recognized until 1952.

The history of sports provides many cases in which creative coaches designed innovative yet legal plays that scored points against a baffled team.
How about the weight room? Can a coach be creative and add some flare
with lifting weights? Absolutely! A few years ago, a student teacher at Lipscomb University had been assigned to a weight lifting class. He observed for
days as the routine of a weight lifting class never varied. With permission,
this student teacher surprised the students one day.

He instructed the class to carry the weights and bars out to the football
field. There the students were divided into teams. A wide variety of games
were played that each involved the carrying of weights. The day's activities
were fun and certainly involved a great deal of strength-building exercises.
The class was undoubtedly long remembered.

The *TGfU* app discussed in chapter 5 shares lesson plans for over two
hundred creatively designed games appropriate for PE classes. With the
variety of activities provided by this single app, far fewer students sit on the
sidelines due to refusing to dress out. The *Fitness Trainer HD* allows students
to take ownership of their own fitness program. The apps in both chapters 6
and 7 are all about creatively addressing the individual needs of each student
through the use of carefully selected apps.

Enhance the Learning Experience

The primary mission of all teachers should be to enhance the learning experience for each student. A great deal of research has focused on strategies
teachers can use to increase the level of learning. Have research projects
shown that iPads do in fact enhance learning? Since iPads were first issued
in 2010, researchers have scrambled to begin longitudinal studies that would
prove or disprove that iPads enhance learning.

However, as researchers know, being able to study and collect data over
time takes years. Add to that the time for publication, and generally three
years is the minimum time needed for sweeping research projects. Since
iPads were first issued in 2010, there has only been time for a limited number
of longitudinal studies. As discussed in the first chapter of the companion

book, *Not a Toy, but a Tool,* a few results began to appear in 2011 and 2012. The four studies mentioned in that book are repeated here, due to the relevance to the discussion of enhancing learning.

A study conducted by the University of Southern California followed 122 elementary students as they worked with the app *Motion Math*. Although the results of that study were specific to only one app, it is representative of thousands of well-designed apps available to educators. Some key findings listed in the executive summary of the study included the following: (1) children's fractions test scores improved an average of over 15 percent; (2) children's self-efficacy for fractions, as well as their liking of fractions, each improved an average of 10 percent; and (3) all participants rated *Motion Math* as fun (Riconscente, 2012, p. 1).

Houghton Mifflin conducted a study with middle school students. The company was testing the effectiveness of their iPad algebra app at Amelia Earhart Middle School in Riverside, CA. Students were randomly selected to use the app and then compared with a control group. "The study showed that 78 percent of students who used the HMH algebra iPad app scored 'proficient' or 'advanced' on the California Standards Test, compared to 59 percent of students who used the textbook version" (Barseghian, 2012). The study also indicated that the students showed an increased interest in algebra.

Certainly, student interest, engagement, and learning are all closely linked. A University of Minnesota study followed a secondary school that had recently purchased three hundred iPads. The devices were given to students for classroom use only. Hwang reported, "students were empowered to learn on their own. Students could shift their role from passive receivers of knowledge to producers of knowledge" (2012).That indeed should be true for every classroom!

Finally, a study from Trinity College in Australia followed groups of college students who were issued iPads for use in any way they found helpful. The academic achievements of those students were compared with the achievements of students who did not use an iPad. The results showed that the "iPad students achieved the highest individual scores" compared to their control group (Jennings, 2012).

All four of those reports indicate a positive relationship between the classroom uses of iPads and the increased learning of the students. Presumably, more studies are ongoing and will continue to be released. However, early indications are that the iPad is a valuable tool for enhancing learning in the classroom.

Reflections on Chapter 1

This chapter has shown the importance of each of the five words that relate to the acronym *DEUCE*. In closing, one might ask "Does the 'and a half' have any significance for iPads?" With the military truck, the expression *deuce and a half* refers to the 2-1/2-ton weight of the truck. Is there any significance for the iPad?

To answer that question, first consider the meaning in today's culture of the expression "and a half." The free app *Urban Dictionary* provides the explanation that "and a half" is used as "an exclamation made by you after someone says something you find particularly true." The example provided in the app is that someone may say, "This ice cream is cold." An appropriate response would be, "And a half!"

So, in closing, imagine a group of educators at a professional development meeting, discussing the effectiveness of the iPad. The conversation might well proceed as follows:

Educator 1: "With the iPad, teachers can use *discovery learning* to achieve a higher level of understanding."

Collective response: "And a half!"

Educator 2: "The iPad *engages students* in ways that no piece of school or classroom technology has ever done."

Collective response: "And a half!"

Educator 3: "Every activity that I initiated with an iPad leads my students to an increased level of *understanding*."

Collective response: "And a half!"

Educator 4: "With the iPad, *creativity* has come into my classrooms, rekindling an interest in learning."

Collective response: "And a half!"

Educator 5: "The iPad *enhances the learning experience* for each of our students!"

Collective response: "And a half!"

This definition of the significance of "and a half" may be a bit contrived. However, there is no doubt that each of the five terms that make up the acronym *DEUCE* has tremendous importance for using the iPad successfully for educational purposes.

Over two hundred apps are included in the following six chapters. Some apps are described with several pages of details. A significant number of other apps are found in lists titled "Additional Highly Rated Apps." Only a few sentences of description accompany those lists, but readers are encouraged to delve further to learn more about those valuable apps.

Finally, some lists include "Previously Discussed Apps." That is, the reader can find fuller descriptions of the apps in other chapters. The five words associated with the acronym *DEUCE* demonstrate the effectiveness and power of each and every one of the apps in this book.

CHAPTER TWO

⸺⟊⟊⟊⸺

Teaching Mathematics
with the iPad

Einstein once commented, "Do not worry about your difficulties in Mathematics. I can assure you mine are still greater." Just imagine if iPads had been around when Einstein lived! Maybe, with the use of an iPad, he would not have experienced those "difficulties." In this chapter, five apps are highlighted in each of the three major areas of elementary, middle, and high school. Additional valuable apps are listed at the end of each section. Altogether, nearly forty apps are mentioned in this chapter. Each app offers valuable techniques for enhancing the learning experience in mathematics.

Math Apps for Elementary School Students (K–4)

Sam Phibian
Recommended Grade Levels: PK and K
Developer: 3CD
Website: 3cd.com
Cost: Free
Common Core Standards Area: Counting and Cardinality

The 3CD website describes this app as, "A cute counting game for preschool to kindergarten-age kids." At the beginning of each game, a student is shown the number of each type of fish that the frog needs to eat. Many little fish and other odd objects swim past a cute frog, but the student is expected to count and only tap the specified numbers. The directions warn that the user should avoid tapping on the wrong object or on more than the specified number of fish. If that is done, the frog grows too big for his lily pad and, sadly, he falls in the water as an alligator appears off to the right.

This app not only gives the student practice with improving counting skills, but it also requires good hand-eye coordination. Supervision to keep a young student on track remains important to check for accuracy. The main problem with this app is that, left alone, a student may begin to think it is fun to watch the frog grow large and sink.

—⁓—

Logic Advanced
Recommended Grade Levels: PK–2
Developer: PopAppFactory
Website: www.popappfactory.com/games/logic2
Cost: $0.99
Common Core Standards Areas: Operations and Algebraic Thinking, Geometry

This app is great for practicing addition and multiplication, as well as roman numerals and basic geometric shapes. The opening screen provides an *Options* button to adjust sound effects and music. Selections can be made for one of five different languages. Tapping the X on the upper right closes that window to select a topic. If, for example, a teacher wants a student to practice multiplication, the teacher can start by tapping on "Count 7 X 8." In the next window, there are ten different multiplication problems.

The answers are at the bottom of the screen, waiting to be dragged and released on top of the correct answer. If that is done correctly, an answer bar pops up momentarily, as shown in figure 2.1. If the answer is incorrect, the answer just falls back to its position as the bottom of the screen. If a student does not know an answer, he or she can tap on the problem, so that the answer bar appears.

In the addition area, the answer is spoken every time the answer bar appears. If preferred, the sound can be muted. A student then has the option to "Play again," which provides a new set of ten problems. All areas are played in the same manner. The "figures" section of this app only requires that the student matches the shapes. Answers such as "Obtuse Triangle," "Sector," or "Trapezoid" appear on the answer bar.

Applications to Other Subjects: Tap on the *Options* button to change the language to Spanish, French, Russian, or Ukrainian. Foreign Language teachers can use this app for practice with those respective languages.

Figure 2.1.   Count Area for Multiplication.
Image created by the author.

—ωωω—

Mathmateer
Recommended Grade Levels: 2–8
Developer: Dan Russell-Pinson
Website: dan-russell-pinson.com/category/games/mathmateer/
Cost: Free or $0.99
Common Core Standards Areas: Operations and Algebraic Thinking, Number and Operations in Base Ten, The Number System, Geometry

Formerly known as *Rocket Math, Mathmateer* has received the Editor's Choice Award from Children's Technology Review in 2011 and remains highly rated on iTunes. The free version of this app does not have quite as many features available, but it is quite sufficient, especially at the elementary level. Teachers of higher grades might prefer to invest in the $0.99 version.

The opening screen has three options: play, select player, and a link to purchase the full version. After tapping on *Select Player*, each player can type in a name and then choose an avatar from a selection of more than a dozen space figures or objects. Once the selections are saved, the next screen allows players to select a new rocket. Then a screen comes up with directions for building a rocket. As parts are added, the student may soon spend all the available money. As a new part is tapped, a message appears asking if the student wants to earn money. If "Yes" is selected, an operation must be selected and then eight math questions appear.

Teachers need to give students ample instructions on how to be successful with building the rocket. Without that instruction, a student may find this app a bit frustrating at first. Teachers should emphasize the importance of balance and thrust. If the boosters and other items are not balanced, the rocket very quickly crashes into the ground. If there is not enough thrust, the rocket cannot reach space, which is where the math missions take place. A sample rocket can be used for beginners, but students usually prefer to build their own.

Before launching a rocket, the "mission" of the endeavor must be selected. The red *New Mission* button for the free version offers a selection of five choices:

- Numbers
- Time
- US Money
- Shapes/Patterns
- Multiply/Divide

A broader range of missions is available on the $0.99 version. When the green *Launch!* button is tapped, the rocket is launched and can be guided by slightly tilting the iPad.

Figure 2.2 shows an example of a rocket that has arrived in space with a mission of US Money. The player should always quickly read the directions at the bottom. In this case, the directions specify that the student should "Tap the coins that add up to 19 cents." Eventually, the rocket falls back to earth. The score, altitude, and air time are all recorded at the top. A student can earn Bronze, Silver, or Gold medals, depending on his or her level of achievement.

The following videos are useful. The first gives an excellent overview of this app. The second video brings out the point that this app also teaches some basic physics principles.

- *Rocket Math:* www.youtube.com/watch?v=ypy-vX2eHKw
- *Rocket Math for the iPad:* www.youtube.com/watch?v=tUmKQSyfFh8

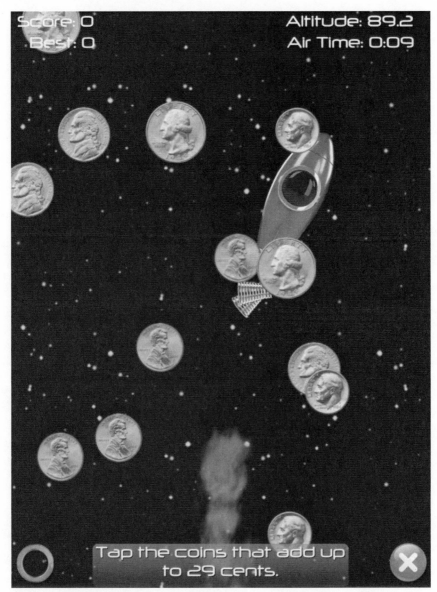

Figure 2.2.   Mathmateer: A Rocket in Space.
Image created by the author.

Applications to Other Subjects: As mentioned previously, this app is also great for science class. Other topics include balance, thrust, angle of inclination, and so on. Awards can be given for the student who achieves the highest altitude.

—⁓—

Fractions by Brainingcamp
Recommended Grade Levels: 3–6
Developer: Brainingcamp, LLC
Website: www.brainingcamp.com
Cost: $0.99
Common Core Standards Areas: Number and Operations—Fractions, The Number System

The *About* page of the Brainingcamp website states that the company is "passionate about making learning a fun and engaging activity." This company focuses only on upper elementary and middle school mathematics products, both for online and mobile devices. The online software costs $10 for two months or $50 for a year. However, they also offer a large collection of effective iPads apps that generally cost $0.99. Because Common Core includes fractions in both the third and fourth grade standards, it is important to include a quality app such as this. This app is highly rated in iTunes and elsewhere.

The opening screen of this app provides seven choices:

- Introduction to Fractions
- Equivalent Fractions
- Common Denominator
- Comparing and Ordering Fractions
- Adding and Subtracting Fractions
- Multiplying Fractions
- Dividing Fractions

After selecting a topic, the user is offered the four choices shown in figure 2.3. Those four areas may be selected in any order, but the lesson is logically the best place to start. That introductory lesson brings up a slideshow presentation, with associated audio explanations. Next, the *Manipulative* section is highly beneficial in providing a student ways to understand the underlying concepts behind fractions. It is important, even essential, for a student to have a basic understanding of fractions, before jumping into the *Questions*

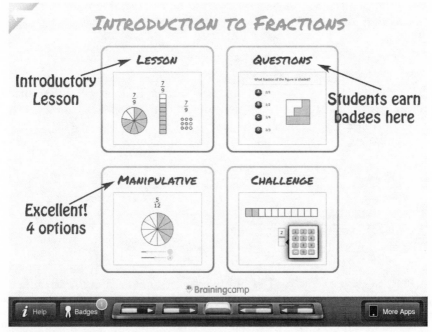

Figure 2.3. Fractions—Basic Concepts.
Image created by the author.

area. In the *Manipulative* section, a student is provided various ways to manipulate factions to see a result.

For example, in the *Manipulative* area of the *Introduction to Fractions*, there are two sliders. As the bottom slider is adjusted, the denominator changes from 1 to 20 sections in a circle. That number corresponds to the dividend in the fraction that is shown. Then, as a student moves the top slider bar, the numerator changes accordingly, up to a maximum of twice the number in the denominator. Initially there is only one circle on the screen, but, as the fraction exceeds the equivalent of 1, two circles appear.

The *Question* area provides ten questions. At any point during the quiz, a student can tap on the small submit button at the bottom and a small chart comes up, which shows the number correct, the number incorrect, and the number unanswered. There is a *Tap to Close* link at the bottom that closes the window. If a question is shown as being wrong, a student can go back and try again. This quiz should be used for practice, not for any summative assessments. A record is kept and badges are awarded each time the ten questions are submitted.

The *Challenge* area is also very important. It is set up very similar to the *Manipulative* area. A student is asked to manipulate the sliders to have the image match the provided fraction. By completing this activity, a student shows that he or she has a good understanding of fractions. For example, if 1/8 is the fraction, the student should move a slider to adjust the number of divisions in a box to 8. Then another slider should be adjusted to show only one of those eight boxes as shaded.

Similarly, if the fraction 15/13, the student can adjust the bottom slider to show to 13 sections in the one rectangle that is provided. However, as the top slider was dragged over to the number 15, two rectangles appear. This is a wonderful way to demonstrate an improper fraction.

—⁓—

Geometry 4 Kids
Recommended Grade Levels: 1–5
Developer: Nth Fusion, LLC
Website: apps.nthfusion.com/geometry4kids.php
Cost: $0.99 (also available on Android)
Common Core Standards Areas: Geometry

Common Core includes geometry as a section of the K–4 standards, so including an app for geometry in this section is imperative. However, trying to find a quality app in this area became problematic. Most apps are too advanced, too expensive, or not highly rated. *Geometry 4 Kids* emerged above a few others because of its excellent collection of illustrations and narratives that can help a young student understand the topics.

One other highly rated app, *Math Geometry*, is listed in *Additional Apps* at the end of this section; it may be preferred, as that app keeps scores and times for each of the five areas. The opening screen for *Geometry for Kids* shows the nine major areas covered:

- Angles and Rays
- Who Am I?—Riddles
- Critical Thinking
- Polygons and Triangles
- Symmetry
- 2D and 3D Shapes
- Transformation and Congruence
- Faces and Sides
- Corners

After tapping on the *Start* button, a student can scroll through the eighteen different selections that include a *Learn* area and a *Practice* area for each of the nine areas. A discussion of the *Learn* and *Practice* areas of 2D Shapes follows; all areas work similarly. After a student taps on *Learn 2D Shapes*, a recording provides an explanation that the section contains a review of twelve different 2D shapes. The little arrow at the bottom right starts another recording with further explanations. A teacher can obviously project this section to the whole class.

If a student is using the app individually, he or she should be provided with earphones so as not to disturb the rest of the class. There are twenty different slides altogether. When finished with one section, a student can tap on a tiny home button at the top left to return to a previous area. Below the home button, a tiny microphone graphic serves as a toggle switch for turning the sound on and off.

After entering the *Practice* area, each slide comes up with the question "What shape is shown?" All odd numbered slides only have the question and a shape showing. However, the following slide always has the answer in a banner below the shape. Again, this can be done for the whole group or for individual students.

———

Additional Highly Rated Apps for Elementary School Math

The following are three other apps that provide excellent learning opportunities for students at the elementary level:

1. *Math Geometry* by Vinta Games, $0.99—This highly rated app has fun figures and a collection of quizzes in five areas (2D shapes, 3D shapes, angles, triangles, and transformations). Unfortunately, there are no sections available to help a student understand the topics prior to taking the quizzes.
2. *Multiplying Acorns—Tasty Math Facts* by Operatio, $2.99—Although it did not make the final cut of five, this is truly an excellent app, providing a lot of opportunities for both fun and learning.
3. *Math Motion: Hungry Fish* by Motion Math, Free—$1.99—Another game app that is cleverly done and highly rated.

Math Apps for Middle School Students (5–8)

This section discusses five of the best mathematics apps for middle school students. The last three apps in the elementary area can also be used at the middle school level. The high school area also discusses some apps that can be used in the upper levels of middle school. So middle school teachers and students should not limit themselves to just reading about the apps in this section.

Math Evolve Lite
Recommended Grade Levels: 5–7
Developer: Zephyr Games
Website: mathevolve.com/
Cost: Free for test. Full version is $1.99 (also available on Android)
Common Core Standards Areas: The Numerical System

The iTunes page for this app mentions several awards, including the statement that this app is "The holy grail of edutainment math apps." Although this app may appear to be too much like an arcade game to be educational, that is exactly the type of game that middle school students crave! They enjoy playing it without realizing how much practice they are getting with their math skills. The game is definitely educational and well worth the time. Every screen has ample practice with arithmetic relationships. Teachers or students can make adjustments in the math levels, as well as the background music.

On the opening screen, a student should type a name and then tap on the *Create* button at the bottom. The next screen is the home screen, with three options: Story Mode, Practice Mode, or Player History. The user should also select a level of math difficulty. The game then asks for a selection of addition, subtraction, multiplication, or division.

This game has levels that a student can move through. The free version only has two levels, but the paid version of this game has twelve levels. After the student taps on *Start Game*, several screens of a story describes the scenario behind the game, as well as the mission of the player. If a student has played the game before, there is an option to skip those screens.

The game section of this app goes quickly, with enemy objects frequently interfering with the mission of solving equations. Those enemy objects need to be shot down. New players should start with the Practice mode, in order to just focus on the equations. Teachers may prefer to use only the practice sessions during class time and leave the gaming features for home. Figure 2.4 is a snapshot of a practice session.

First, a question flashes on the screen, such as "59 + 73" and then the possible answers float down. When a student drags over the correct answer, a large checkmark appears. A wrong answer brings up a big X and the play stops as a new screen asks the student, "What's the correct answer?" The student can tap on the provided keypad. When the corrected answer is entered,

Figure 2.4. Math Evolve, Game in Progress.
Image created by the author.

the practice session resumes. Another benefit of the paid version of this game is that there is a history section, where teachers can check a student's achievements.

This video shows some additional features: www.youtube.com/watch?v =7eAn3meBUpg

---

Middle School Math 7th Grade
Recommended Grade Levels: 6–8
Developer: Monkey in the Middle Apps, LLC
Website: monkeyinthemiddleapps.com/
Cost: Free, but $1.99 recommended (also available on Android)
Common Core Standards Areas: The Numerical System, Proportions and Ratios, Statistics and Probability

Gaming features are still present with this app, but there are far more categories than with the previous app. The opening screen lists the twelve categories available in the paid version of this app. For the free version, only the following four are available:

- Negative Numbers (Addition and Subtraction)
- Negative Numbers (Multiplication and Division)
- Absolute Value
- Order of Operations

The remaining eight areas are provided with the $1.99 version:

- Fractions (Addition and Subtraction)
- Fractions (Multiplication and Division)
- Decimals
- Scientific Notation
- Percentages
- Factors and Multiples
- Ratios and Proportions
- Probability

Once a category is selected, a screen comes up similar to the image in figure 2.5. The player needs to tilt the iPad to let the monkey slide over to the closest ladder and, ultimately, get him to the bottom of the screen. During that activity, an assortment of multiple-choice math problems comes up that freeze

Figure 2.5. Middle School Math, 7th Grade: Game in Progress.
Image created by the author.

the monkey's motion until the problem is answered. If the answer is correct, it appears green and the problem slides off the screen. Then the monkey resumes his decent. In addition, bananas are earned for correct answers.

However, if the answer is wrong, the chosen answer is shown in red and the correct one is green. As the question window slides off, the monkey jumps back up to the previous row as a penalty for being wrong, before being able to resume his descent. Soon another question appears. Every time a game is completed, a sheet comes up showing the number of correct answers, the total time played, and a list of all the questions. As the game proceeds, bananas are accumulated for the monkey in the upper right corner.

This app also includes flashcards and five other "games" in each category. The paid version of this app has an excellent selection of twelve different topics. In the Probability section, one question is, "If the weatherman says there is a 30% chance of rain. . . ." Possible answers are, "It is raining," "It will rain," "It might rain," and "It will not rain." Another question is, "Probability of rolling a 2 on a 6 sided die, . . ." with possible answers of 2/6, 1/6, 1/2, and 1/3. All the questions associated with this app are appropriate for middle school math.

—◦◦◦—

Geoboard, by The Math Learning Center
Recommended Grade Levels: 5–8
Developer: Clarity Innovations
Website: catalog.mathlearningcenter.org/apps/geoboard
Cost: Free
Common Core Standards Areas: Geometry

The following information is available by tapping on the *i* at the bottom right: "Learners stretch bands around pegs to form line segments and polygons and make discoveries about perimeter, area, angles, congruence, fractions, and more." Certainly, many teachers have a Geoboard, but imagine how wonderful it would be to have a virtual Geoboard without having to worry about rubber bands flying across the room!

On this virtual Geoboard, a student can choose from eight different colors of bands. Those bands can then be stretched over pegs to make the various geometric shapes. The first board has twenty-five pegs. However, there is a small, faded icon with an arrow in the upper right. Drag that icon in the direction of the arrow, and the board changes to a board with 150 pegs. Similarly, a student can return to the board with fewer pegs by dragging the icon that is now on the upper left.

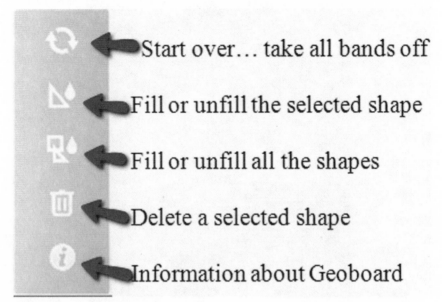

Start over... take all bands off

Fill or unfill the selected shape

Fill or unfill all the shapes

Delete a selected shape

Information about Geoboard

Figure 2.6.   Geoboard Tools.
Image created by the author.

At the bottom of the screen are five icons, as shown in figure 2.6. Teachers can write lesson plans that use this app the same way a regular Geoboard would be used. For example, one lesson might simply ask a student to make a series of specified shapes. Another lesson would allow the students to discover the areas of various shapes by using the area between four pegs as the unit. Then a student can be asked how many unit areas are within the shape or shapes they have on the board. Perimeters can also be studied with this app.

Clarity Innovation has an excellent support site where a teacher or student can send questions to the developers (www.clarity-innovations.com/apps).

———❦❦❦———

Middle School Algebra
Recommended Grade Levels: 7–9
Developer: Monkey in the Middle Apps, LLC
Website: monkeyinthemiddleapps.com/
Cost: Free, but $0.99 version is recommended (also available on Android)
Common Core Standards Areas: Creating Equations, Inequalities, Exponential Models

This is the same company that designed the *Middle School Math 7th Grade* app with the energetic monkey. The functioning of the game is very similar,

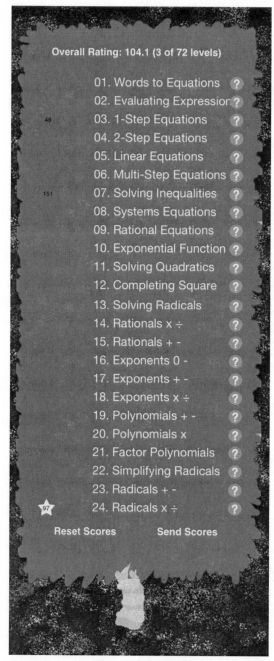

Figure 2.7. Topics for Middle School Algebra (Algebra Pro).
Image created by the author.

but the topics are significantly different; in all, twenty-four topics are available, as shown in figure 2.7. The other major difference is that the monkey is jumping up to different levels, rather than sliding down. For this game, the iPad should only be titled slightly, certainly not nearly as much as with the sliding-down monkey. Only slight movements seem to have a significant effect.

The questions are excellent for improving student skills in the ten different areas. As with the *Middle School Math 7th Grade* app, the free version of this app only provides access to the first four topics. The Pro version has twenty-four different topics. The scores from these "games" can be sent back to the teacher.

Test Review Pre-Algebra Master
Recommended Grade Levels: 7–8
Developer: WebMetrics Software
Website: www.webmetricssoftware.com/PreAlgebraMaster.html
Cost: $0.99
Common Core Standards Areas: Ratios and Proportional Relationships, The Number System, Expressions and Equations

With repeated searches, both the preceding app by Monkey in the Middle and this app come up as one of the best low-cost apps for pre-algebra. These apps work well as partners, because they are a bit different in their approach. *Middle School Algebra* by Monkey in the Middle is, of course, a game, although teaching concepts are definitely part of the mission. This app is more straightforward and traditional in its approach. The benefit of using this app is that wrong answers are explained. Rather than just being given the correct answer, an explanation of the solution is provided.

The home screen for this app is very bland, including a list of the various sections:

- Practice
- Study
- Test
- Time Trails
- Flashcards
- Instructions
- Load
- Settings

That is a nice collection of categories for an inexpensive app. The instructions should be read first to become familiar with the assortment of icons used throughout the various sections. Note that, throughout the program, the Back bar is always at the top. Each of the first five selections of the homepage (*Practice, Study, Test, Time Trails, Flashcards*) provides a choice of eight related topics. Those eight topics are:

- Numbers
- Expressions
- Equations
- Word Problems
- Decimals and Fractions
- Graphs
- Polynomials
- Principles of Mathematics

Any combination of those topics can be selected. The *Start* button is located at the top. The *Study* area provides the answer and also shows the steps needed to obtain that answer. Throughout the collection of problems, for the *Practice, Test,* or *Time Trails,* a student needs to tap on the answer at the bottom of the page, rather than next to the problem itself. In the *Practice* section, students can see whether their answer is correct.

Whether an answer is correct or not, a solution is provided. For example, one problem asks students to solve the following equation: $(x - 1)/2 = (x - 2)/3$. Students may select from possible answers, as follows: $x = 1$, $x = -1$, $x = 2$, or $x = -2$. For this problem, the correct answer is -1. After the student selects an answer, the solution is shown below the answer, as follows: $(x - 1)/2 = (x - 2)/3$, then we cross multiply to get $3(x - 1) = 2(x - 2)$, $3x - 3 = 2x - 4$, so $x = -1$. The app also shows the students the number of problems that have been answered correctly, compared with the total problems attempted. An example of both a correct and an incorrect solution is shown in figure 2.8.

At the end of the session, an overview is provided that shows all the questions in a format as shown previously, along with the times needed to finish each problem. A percent score is also be shown. Overall, this is an app that can be used for projecting from a single iPad and just as easily in one-to-one classrooms, where each student can practice independently.

Additional Highly Rated App for Middle School Math

Chicken Coop Fractions Game by Lumpty Learning for grades 5–8, Free (also available on Android)—This is a delightful, MUST SEE app! Trying to write

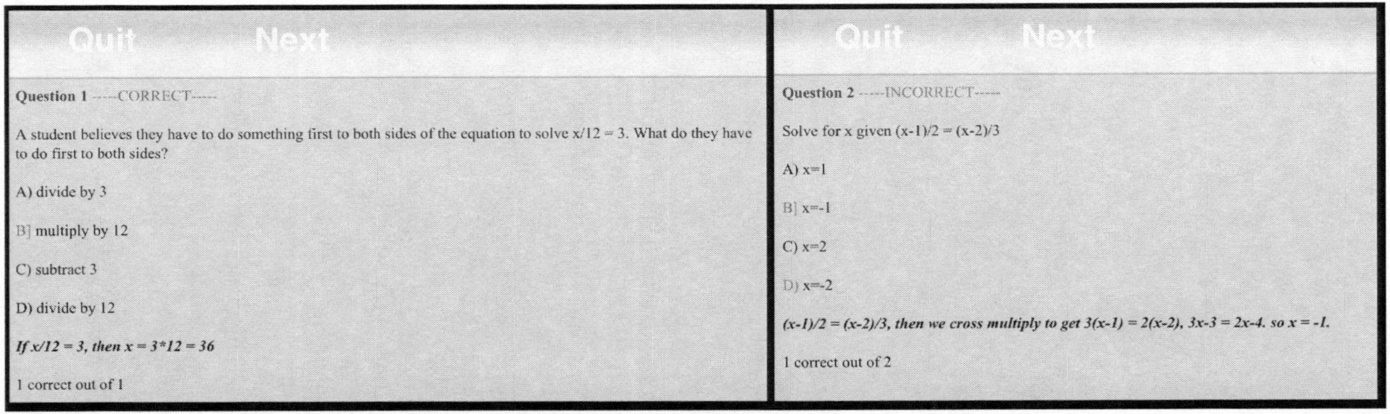
Quit
Next
Question 1 -----CORRECT-----
A student believes they have to do something first to both sides of the equation to solve x/12 = 3. What do they have to do first to both sides?
A) divide by 3
B] multiply by 12
C) subtract 3
D) divide by 12
If x/12 = 3, then x = 3*12 = 36
1 correct out of 1
Quit
Next
Question 2 -----INCORRECT-----
Solve for x given (x-1)/2 = (x-2)/3
A) x=1
B] x=-1
C) x=2
D) x=-2
(x-1)/2 = (x-2)/3, then we cross multiply to get 3(x-1) = 2(x-2), 3x-3 = 2x-4. so x = -1.
1 correct out of 2

Figure 2.8. Examples of Correct and Incorrect Answers in Practice Section.
Image created by the author.

too much about this app would steal some of the pleasure of seeing the app play through for the first time. The focus, throughout the app, is on estimating fractions. This app develops an understanding of fractions, including improper fractions.

The topics build from the "easy" to "hard" levels, including allowing a student one minute to estimate the decimal value of a collection of "hard" improper fractions. To provide any further instructions would only spoil the surprise. Have fun! And do not miss seeing the chickens hatch at the end of each game.

Math Apps for High School Students (9–12)

Selecting math apps for high school was a more difficult endeavor than it was for the lower grades. Part of the reason is that many of the quality apps are priced higher than the $1.99 limit set for this book. Then there is the additional problem of having such a wide range of math subjects at the high school level. Whereas so much of elementary mathematics is just learning the basics of arithmetic, high school subjects run the gamut of pre-algebra, algebra I, algebra II, geometry, trigonometry, statistics and probability, pre-calculus, and calculus. All told, eight different subjects are prevalent at the high school level.

In addition to covering apps for those eight areas, a calculator app also needs to be recommended, bringing the total to nine, but the space is limited in this book! Pre-algebra is addressed in the middle school section, so that gets the list back down to eight. Combining pre-calculus and calculus, as well as algebra I and II, still leaves six. Only five are included for high school, but the last app includes areas for both algebra and statistics. However, a fairly extensive *Additional Highly Rated Apps* section is included at the end of this section. Although trigonometry is not covered within the five apps, it is covered in the final listing of apps.

Calculator for iPad Free
Recommended Grade Levels: 5–10
Developer: International Travel Weather Calculator
Website: www.itwcalculator.com/
Cost: Free or $1.99 for Pro

Deciding on a calculator app also led to problems. Quite a few quality apps serve the role of calculator. Some are just basic calculators with limited frills, and then there are the math-lover's calculators with functions replicating the hand-held scientific calculators. This app was chosen because its features meet the needs of the majority of algebra and geometry students.

If a math-phobic student is required to use a scientific calculator, with all its bells and whistles, the experience will likely only exacerbate the fear of math. Although *Calculator for iPad Pro* is described here, six other calculator apps are of high quality and are described in the listings at the end of this section.

According to the International Travel Weather Calculator website, this app is "the original calculator for iPad." Of course being the original one of a large group of calculator apps does not necessarily make it the best. However, the ease with which this calculator can be used gives it an advantage over other apps. It is quite intuitive. While holding the iPad vertically, the calculator offers just the simplest of functions.

If, however, the iPad is switched to the horizontal position, the other options shown on the left of the image become available. The app has the functions that most students need through algebra 1 and geometry. As mentioned before, teachers should check out the six other calculator apps in the *Additional Highly Rated Apps* section at the end of this chapter. Some of those include more advanced features.

—ᴧᴧ—

Math App—Geometry 1
Recommended Grade Levels: 7–11
Developer: Digital Brainwash
Website: www.digitalbrainwash.com/
Cost: Free or $0.99
Common Core Standards Areas: Geometry, Similarity, Right Triangles and
    Trigonometry, Modeling with Geometry

This app does not cover a broad range of geometry topics, but instead simply focuses on information about various polygons. The home screen has drawings of five triangles (equilateral, right, isosceles, acute and obtuse). Tapping on any of those brings up a small screen that gives the definition of the specific triangle, as well as additional facts that apply to that triangle. In some cases, there are links to a second screen with more information.

For example, the definition screen for right triangles has a link to a screen with more information on the Pythagorean theorem. At the bottom of the screen there are five different selections:

- Triangles
- Quadrilaterals

- Circle
- Other
- Settings

The first three areas show related figures, as well as a chart that relates to quiz scores. *Quadrilaterals*, for example, show images of a rectangle, square, parallelogram, rhombus, and trapezoid. Each figure has sides and angles labeled. The parallelogram has an arrow indicating the parallel sides.

Below the chart of quiz scores, a *Take Quiz* button opens the quiz area with some multiple choice questions and some questions requiring exact answers. After each correct answer is submitted, a student hears a cheer, unless the sound has been muted. After a student finishes a quiz, a gold trophy appears, along with the score. The student is then asked to enter a name, so that the scores are recorded.

The *Settings* area is where the teacher can mute the sounds, as well as set the number of questions and also the time allowed for each question. There is also a link to *View High Scores*. Up to twenty scores are retained. On the bottom of the screen, there is also an *Other* link, which goes to a *More Stuff* page. A student can access information for one- to ten-sided polygons. There are also a *Formulas Quick Sheet* and a *Master Test* link.

Several other iPad apps cover a broader area of the topics, but they all cost more. A selection of several other geometry apps is included in the *Additional Valuable Apps* section.

⟶⟋⟋⟍⟍⟋⟍⟶

Algebra Touch
Recommended Grade Levels: 7–11
Developer: Regular Berry Software, LLC
Website: www.regularberry.com/
Cost: $2.99
Common Core Standards Areas: Creating Equations, Reasoning with Equations and Inequalities

This is a "Must See" app for every teacher who teaches about algebraic expressions! Unfortunately, the cost is above my stated cut-off price of $1.99, due to an increase in price after the original writing of this chapter. However, the price is worth the fee, particularly if a teacher is using only one iPad. A teacher can project from the iPad to show the various features. This is app is extremely popular with students and teachers alike.

When the app is first opened, the topic of addition is selected by default. Tap on the addition sign to have the sum appear. This section of the app can be used for very young children. However, the purpose of the low-level sections is simply to begin to get student comfortable with how the various functions work. Operating this app is not intuitive, but, once the techniques become familiar, it becomes engaging for students and fun to use.

The app allows a student to both practice problems and also to read explanations. For example, if the student selects *Basic Equations* from the *Lessons* drop down menu on the left of the top menu bar, one of the screens may show an equation like the one shown in figure 2.9. The *Explain* button has been selected, at the top. If a student prefers to select the *Practice* button, then the same equations appears, without the explanations in the white area at the bottom.

The word *Touch* was given to this app, as touching is used to solve problems. For example, in the previous problem, a student can tap the plus sign on each side and watch the equation change to 6x = 12. There are two ways to solve the problem. The easiest way is to simply tap on 6x to change it to 6
• x. Then the student can drag the 6 to the denominator on the other side.

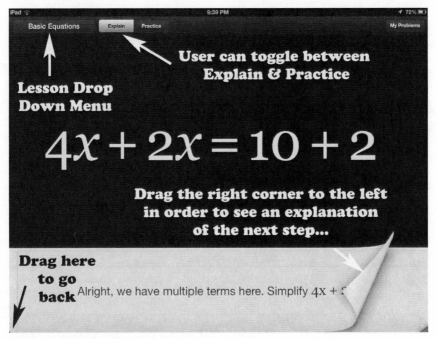

Figure 2.9. Algebra Touch: Basic Equations Screen.
Image created by the author.

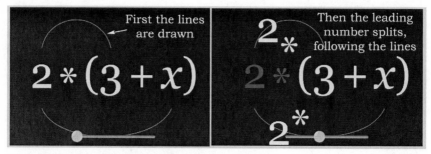

Figure 2.10.   Showing Distribution in Action with Algebra Touch.
Image created by the author.

Realizing that the fraction needs to be reduced, the student should tap on the 12, which shows in blue two selections: 3 • 4 or 2 • 6. After the student taps on 2 • 6, he or she can tap and drag an imaginary line through the two 6s. As the student drags his or her finger, a red line appears and the 6s disappear, thus leaving the answer of x = 2. Other longer methods for solving the equation can also be used.

The app has a impressive technique for using the Distributive law. With the equation shown in figure 2.10, a student has tapped on the • after –2. Thin blue lines then appear, along with the slider at the bottom. As the student drags the slider to the right, the –2 begins to slowly distribute along the lines, until the following equation shows: –2 • 14 + –2 • 4y = 18 + 15y.

Four important buttons are at the top right the screen. The *Undo* button allows a student to undo any step that he or she felt was wrong. The *Restart* button returns the user to the beginning of the problem. The *Random* button varies the level of difficulty of the problems. The *My Problems* button allows students to create their own equations as part of a set.

The video at the company's website is useful when learning how to use the app. Also check out this fairly recent YouTube video: www.youtube.com/watch?v=-6Uz9Gj2Ln0.

————〰————

Video Calculus
Recommended Grade Levels: 11–12
Developer: Thinkwell
Website: www.thinkwell.com/
Cost: Free for only fifteen videos

This app provides a large collection of videos that are superb for introducing a topic and also for reinforcing initial presentations. In addition, they are particularly ideal for the flipped classroom. In the *Description* area on the iTunes page, L. McMullin, a reviewer from the College Board, writes that this app has "the best Calculus lessons this reviewer has seen anywhere." In the free version, fifteen videos in the *Featured* category are available in their entirety:

- The Two Questions of Calculus
- Finding Limits Graphically
- Limits and Indeterminate Forms
- Finding Instantaneous Velocity
- The Derivative
- A Shortcut for Finding Derivatives
- The Product Rule
- The Can Problem
- The Peddle Problem
- Gravity and Vertical Motion
- Calculus I in 20 Minutes
- An Introduction to l'Hôpital's Rule
- Differentiating Logarithmic Functions
- An Introduction to the Integral Table
- An Introduction to Integration by Parts

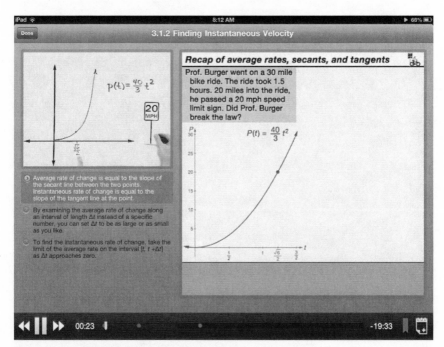

Figure 2.11. Video Calculus: Typical Layout of the Videos.
Image created by the author.

Video Calculus also offers a vast collection of other videos, but only the first minute of those videos are available within the free version. For those who have paid for the full app, there are twenty-two different sections and each section has anywhere from one to forty-five different videos. The fee structure varies from $4.99 for a 30-day pass to $19.99 for a 360-day pass. Most of the videos are approximately ten minutes in length, but some are over twenty minutes.

Figure 2.11 shows a sample of one of the videos. In the left window, an instructor is explaining the topic, as he draws on the graph and adds various figures, such as the 20 mph sign. That screen area is also used to show how equations are developed and solved. Below that screen are some bullet points about the presentation. Then the right area has more presentation-style graphics. This is an excellent app. If the money is available, this app offers an extensive collection of excellent videos.

———⁂———

PrepZilla Study with Friends Test Prep Game
Recommended Grade Levels: 8–12
Developer: gWhiz, LLC
Website: www.regularberry.com/
Cost: Free or additional features for fees
Common Core Standards Areas: Grade 8, Fractions; Algebra, Equations; Statistics and Probability

This is another free and highly rated app, with additional features available for purchase. After tapping on the *Select Topic* button at the lower left, a list of forty-eight different subjects is provided. Five of the available topics are within the area of mathematics:

- Algebra I
- Fractions—Volume 1
- Basic Math—Volume 1
- AP Statistics
- AP Calculus

When a topic is selected, the user is brought back to the main screen, where a choice can be made to either study alone with the *Self-Study* button, or to study with other students with the *Who Knows?* button. In the *Self-Study* section, a list of categories is provided. A practice quiz is generated with questions from the various categories selected by the user. As shown in figure 2.12, there is also a *Get More Questions* button at the top. Tapping

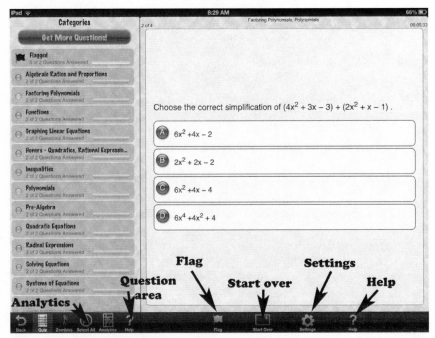

Figure 2.12. Sample PrepZilla Quiz Question.
Image created by the author.

there opens a new window with the fee for purchasing more questions. For example, $4.99 purchases over 400 Algebra I questions or $8.99 buys 450 AP Calculus AS/BC questions.

Once the topic and categories have been selected, a student should tap on the *Quiz* icon at the bottom. As the student proceeds through the quiz, tapping on the *Flag* icon at the bottom of the screen saves any of the problems for later review. When the practice quiz is finished, a small window pops up that provides the overview of the right and wrong answers, as well as any flagged questions. After tapping *Okay* on that small screen, every question is provided, with the correct and incorrect answers marked. Along with each correct answer, there is an explanation about how the answer was derived.

The *Filter* icon and the *Results* icon, shown in figure 2.13, are new icons that become available on the bottom menu only after a quiz is completed. When reviewing answers, a student can tap on the *Filter* icon at the bottom to select only the wrong or flagged answers. Tapping on the *Results* icon brings up the quick overview again.

Tapping on the *Analytics* icon gives the student four options:

- Statistics
- Strength by Category

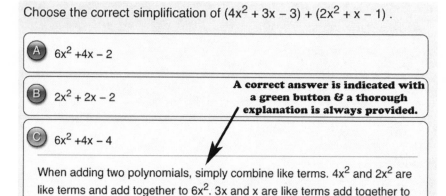

Choose the correct simplification of $(4x^2 + 3x - 3) + (2x^2 + x - 1)$.

A $6x^2 + 4x - 2$

B $2x^2 + 2x - 2$

A correct answer is indicated with a green button & a thorough explanation is always provided.

C $6x^2 + 4x - 4$

When adding two polynomials, simply combine like terms. $4x^2$ and $2x^2$ are like terms and add together to $6x^2$. $3x$ and x are like terms add together to $4x$. The constants -3 and -1 add together to -4. The final answer is $6x^2 + 4x - 4$.

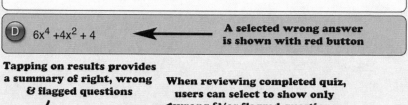

D $6x^4 + 4x^2 + 4$

A selected wrong answer is shown with red button

Tapping on results provides a summary of right, wrong & flagged questions

When reviewing completed quiz, users can select to show only wrong &/or flagged questions.

Same throughout

Results · Filter · Flag · Start Over · Settings · Help

Figure 2.13.   Reviewing Answers with PrepZilla.
Image created by the author.

- Quiz History
- Clear Test Results

The first three can only be used when more than one quiz has been taken, but it is valuable information for teachers and students alike. The *Clear* option is especially useful when the iPad is being shared.

The *Who Knows* section is the fun area where students can study with their friends. Logging in can be done either with Facebook or with a user name and e-mail address. To start a new game, a student should tap on the plus icon at the bottom. Up to three players can be added. The screen also needs to have the topic selected, as well as the number of questions and the seconds allowed per questions. The participants simply take turns answering the questions.

And, oh yes, do not miss the cute little fire-breathing dragon that stands by the *Select Topics* button. Occasionally it holds up a banner to inform a user about additional options.

Applications to Other Subjects: As mentioned previously, there are forty-eight different subjects with this app. There are many subjects in the area of English and history. Chemistry and physics are also included, as well as Spanish.

Additional Highly Rated Apps for High School Math

This High School Math area has more additional apps than any other section in this book. All these apps have features that can help teachers promote student learning in one or more areas of mathematics.

Calculators
1. *Quick Graph: Your Scientific Graphing Calculator* by Colombianmug, Free
2. *Free Graphing Calculator* by William Jockuach, Free
3. *Convert Any Unit Free—Units & Currency Converter & Calculator* by Cider Software, LLC, Free
4. *CalcMadeEasy Free—Scientific Calculator with Automatic Notes* by Lalit Patil, Free
5. *Calculator#*, Free, and *Calculator∞*, $2.99, both by Incpt.Mobis— These are both very highly rated. The free version was not included in the top five areas, simple in deference to the math-phobic student. For AP classes, this is great!
6. *TI-Nspire* and *TI-Nspire CAS* by Texas Instruments Incorporated, both $29.99—Highly rated and an incredibly low price, compared with the purchase price of the actual TI-Nspire!

Algebra
1. *Khan Academy—Algebra I* by Khan Academy, Free (also available on Android)—This is not an new app, but rather is included here as a reminder. See chapter 3 of the companion book, *Not a Toy, but a Tool* for a full description. The app has awesome videos for all math areas.
2. *Hands-On Equations (Level 1 Lite)* by Hands on Equations, Free, with more upgrades for $3.99 or $4.99 (also available on Android)—This is a highly rated app, with both videos and practice problems.
3. *Algebra II* and *Vector Algebra* by WAGmob, $1.99 (also available on Android)—No ratings are available, but this seems to be an excellent app covering a broad range of Algebra II topics.
4. *WolframAlpha* by Wolfram Alpha, LLC, $2.99 (also available on Android)—This app is amazing, valuable, and worth the price. It includes solutions to complex equations such as complicated integrals or cubic

equations. Steps are provided, as well as graphs. The price is the only reason this app was not selected for a more detailed discussion.

5. *HMH Fuse: Algebra I/Algebra II, Common Core* by Houghton Mifflin Harcourt, Free—This app is a companion to Houghton Mifflin Harcourt's algebra I textbook. The app comes with a free sample chapter, along with other features. The Common Core version of the algebra app is more highly rated than the original algebra I versions. Both algebra II and geometry also have a Common Core version.

6. *Algebra Champ* by Brian West, Free—This is a very simple and fun game with three levels of difficulty. The main disadvantage is that there are no explanations for wrong answers.

7. *MathBot—TeX Equation Typesetting* by wiApps, Free with upgrade available for $4.99—This apps provides a way to create and copy complex math equations. It does require learning TeX typesetting codes, but the equations have a professional appearance.

Geometry and Trigonometry

1. *Unit Circle* by Hugo Masclet, $0.99—Helps students understand basic characteristics of a circle, including sine, cosine, and tangent.

2. *Video Geometry Tutor* by iPREPpress LLC, $1.99 (also available on Android)—This highly rated app is an awesome collection of videos, and is an excellent way to introduce key topics.

3. *Geometry* by YourTeacher.com, $9.99 (available on Android)—This is probably the best app in this category, in my opinion. However, it was delegated to this area because of the price.

4. *ACT Math: Geometry Lite* by Webrich Software Limited/Eknath Kadam, Free for some sections or $1.99 for full version (available on Android)—This app has good practice problems.

5. *Math GMAT GRE ACT Prep Game* by NKO Ventures, LLC, Free—This app is highly rated.

6. *Trigonometry Help—Triangle Calculator + Formulae* by David Caddy, $1.99—This is an excellent app for understanding the relationships between the sides and angles of a triangle. This can be used in geometry.

Statistics

1. *Statistics Visualizer* by Miaoshuang Dong, Free—This app has excellent graphs, a statistical calculator, and detailed explanations.

2. *Wolfram Statistics Course Assistant* by Wolffram Alpha, LLC, $2.99 (available on Android)—Again, Wolfram provides quality math apps, but the price limits their selection in the regular areas of this chapter

Calculus

1. *Calculus Pro* by Larry Feldman, $0.99 (also available on Android)— This app contains a collection of examples and tutorials that cover a wide range of calculus topics.
2. *Calculus FTW—Deep Insight into Solving Calculus Problems* by MathFTW, LLC, $2.99—This app includes step-by-step solutions to hundreds of problems. The focus is on first-year calculus.

Reflections on Chapter 2

More apps are included in this chapter on mathematics than in any other chapter of this book, primarily because of the great number of different subjects that all fall under the umbrella of mathematics. The forty-two apps described or listed in this chapter provide a valuable box of tools for any math teacher. Each of these apps can transform the mathematics classroom through the use of the *DEUCE* technique, as discussed in chapter 1. One carefully chosen app at a time can bring a spark of joy and excitement into all levels of mathematics instruction.

—•◦•—

CHAPTER THREE

Teaching Science
with the iPad

Isaac Asimov, the prolific writer of popular science fiction books, once said, "The most exciting phrase to hear in science, the one that heralds new discoveries, is not 'Eureka!' (I found it!), but 'That's funny'" (Wainer and Lysen, 2009). Full understanding of a scientific concept is often preceded by a sense of confusion. With the confusion may indeed come the thought, "That's funny."

In science, thinking that something is "funny" conveys surprise; a new understanding follows. Each of the apps in this chapter was selected for its ability to offer students either a sense of discovery or a sense of surprise. Apps that just list facts or equations were avoided. All of the following apps can assist teachers in their efforts to maximize student engagement by making science both fun and "funny."

Science Apps for
Elementary School Students (K–4)

Ansel & Clair: Jurassic Dinosaurs
Recommended Grade Levels: 2–4
Developer: Cognitive Kid, Inc.
Website: www.anselandclair.com/
Cost: $1.99

Unquestionably, dinosaurs fascinate nearly every elementary student. This app does an excellent job of turning learning into a fun activity. Altogether a substantial amount of information is included covering seven different dinosaurs. The opening screen requests that the name of the player be chosen or typed. Four different students can register on one iPad. The next screen explains how this "game" is played.

Ansel and Clair are the key characters; they have flown to earth from another planet to learn about dinosaurs. They travel on a spaceship named Marley. In figure 3.1, Claire hovers above Ansel who is more grounded. Throughout their travels, they always have access to three tools: a camera, a travel log, and a tracker that lets a student play and replay each of the many recordings that are provided.

The first scene explains to the student how to maneuver through the various features of this app. The second scene allows the student to learn a bit about how paleontologists find fossils. Throughout the app, a blue hand points to where the student should tap to achieve a task or go to a subsequent screen. On the third scene, Ansel and Clair begin their travel back in time. They briefly hover above the earth to gaze at how the earth might have looked during the time of the dinosaurs. Next, they move on to study the

Figure 3.1. Ansel & Clair Visit the Jurassic Period.
Image created by the author.

dinosaurs from the Jurassic period. That scene is the primary area for learning about each of the dinosaurs, including:

- Hybodus
- Stegosaurus
- Allosaurus
- Plesiosaurus
- Brachiosaurus
- Archeopteryx
- Apatosaurus

Even information about pine trees is included. As every dinosaur is mentioned, the student is encouraged to take a picture with the camera tool. Those pictures are stored to be used in the journal. After hearing the information about a dinosaur, teachers can make sure that the student has taken a picture; then the student can proceed to the journal area.

A student can scroll through the journal area by swiping left or right on the top of the pages. The pictures the student has taken are off to the right side of the journal page. The student can drag the picture to the top of the page and then write the information about the dinosaur. When the student taps on the purse, a snapshot is taken of the journal page. An e-mail automatically pops up with the image attached. The student can then e-mail his or her journal page to the teacher. Another area of the app allows a student to create his or her own dinosaur.

Certainly, for an elementary student, the names of the dinosaurs are difficult. For that reason, this app may be best for the upper elementary grades. Also, the activities should be spread over several days. Older teachers may be surprised to learn from this app that the Brontosaurus dinosaur is mere fiction and never existed. Decades ago, the existence of the Brontosaurus was routinely taught in schools. As explained on the app, the dinosaur that was thought to be a Brontosaurus was really just an Apatosaurus. The issue was not resolved until the 1970s.

——ʘʘʘ——

Additional Highly Rated Apps by the Same Designer
Teachers and students who enjoy this app might also want to check out two other equally engaging apps:

- *Ansel & Clair: Triassic Dinosaurs*, $1.99
- *Ansel & Clair: Cretaceous Dinosaurs*, $1.99

—◄◦◢◦►—

3rd Grade 4th Grade Life Science Reading Comprehension
Recommended Grade Levels: 3–4
Developer: Abitalk Incorporated
Website: www.abitalk.com/
Cost: Free for four stories; additional sixteen stories for $2.99

The ability not only to read, but to comprehend what one is reading is undoubtedly one of the most important skills to acquire for success both in school and in society in general. This free app provides four stories that assess student understanding of scientific topics. The opening screen encourages viewers to upgrade to the full version with sixteen stories, but educators can work with the first four stories and then decide whether to invest the extra funds. To get started, simply tap on *Guest*. The next screen offers three links: *Reading Comprehension, Self-Created Lessons,* and *Create Your Own Lessons*.

If *Reading Comprehension* is selected, the following four readings are available with the free app:

- Biological Organizations
- Classifying and Naming Living Things
- Cell Structure and Function I
- Cell Structure and Function II

The graphics and pictures are interspersed throughout the readings of all areas of this app to assist students with their understanding of the topics under discussion. Every word in the readings area can be tapped to hear the correct pronunciation. That feature separates this app from so many others that only have relatively few words linked to a recording. A student with lower reading abilities can significantly benefit from that attribute. At the bottom of each screen is a question.

For example, the following is the first question in the *Classifying and Naming Living Things* area, along with the possible answers:

Today, how do scientists group organisms into categories?

- Based on their size
- Based on where they live on Earth
- Based on how closely related they are
- Based on how they look

If a student gets the correct answer, a happy face is shown. For wrong answers, there is an unhappy face. A student can try repeatedly until the correct answer is obtained. After answering all the questions, a student should tap on the submit button at the top right, which brings up the *Report* area. For each story, the report shows the number of questions that were correct, separated by type of question.

Teachers should be aware that a student might skip reading the story and just tap the answers until he or she gets the correct response. Regardless, this app has tremendous value for giving a student practice with reading. If the activity is used at home, it can serve as a study aid prior to a test. If used in the classroom, the students can show each report to the teacher. The teacher can then tap on the reset button to have the app ready for another class.

Applications to Other Subjects: This also has value for English Language Learner (ELL) classes. The feature that allows a student to tap on any word to hear the correct pronunciation is a tremendous feature, particularly for an ELL student.

——⁓⁓——

A *Life Cycle App*
Recommended Grade Levels: 3–4
Developer: Nth Fusion LLC
Website: apps.nthfusion.com/
Cost: $0.99 (also available on Android)

The opening screen summarizes the app's focus on learning various growth stages through self-paced, interactive learning. After tapping on *Begin,* the next screen provides the following twelve topics:

- Life Cycle of a Frog
- Phases of the Moon
- Life Cycle of a Butterfly
- Plant Life Cycle
- Pollution and Fertilization
- Rock Cycle
- Water Cycle
- Photosynthesis
- Nitrogen Cycle
- Oxygen Cycle

- Ladybug
- Question Time

This app works equally well as a learning tool for individual students or for projection for whole-class instruction. All areas work similarly. Figure 3.2 shows the sixth screen within the *Life Cycle of a Frog*. The first screen gives an overview of the cycle. Tap anywhere and the background turns black and a recording begins that explains the cycle. Each tap explains the succeeding stage.

If the teacher wants a student to read the information without the recording, the microphone in the upper left area serves as a toggle switch for turning the recording on or off. Similarly, if a teacher is showing the images to a whole class and does not want the textbox to show, the large letter *T* closes the textbox.

The last area is the *Question Time*. Unfortunately, this only provides questions for the *Life Cycle of the Frog*. As the student views the question, along with four possible answers, a recording provides a reading of the question. The recording can also be muted if a teacher wishes. The next screen that follows the question screen provides the correct answer. These ques-

Figure 3.2. Life Cycle of a Frog.
Image created by the author.

tions should be used more for student practice, rather than for any formal assessment. There is a considerable amount of good scientific information with this one app. It can be used at various times throughout a year's science curriculum.

—⁓—

Kid Weather
Recommended Grade Levels: K–2
Developer: Just in Weather
Website: kidweatherapp.com/
Cost: $1.99 (also available on Android)

To begin working with this app, a student firsts need to pick an avatar, selecting either male or female, as well as human, dog, or cat. For a selection of female and human, the screen brings up the figure similar to the one shown in figure 3.3. Her attire changes depending on the current outside weather, with the background reflecting the time of day. The current temperature and location are shown at the top. On the left side, tapping on the clock icon brings up three choices: *Current Weather, Later Today,* and *Tomorrow's High. Current Weather* is the default setting, but tapping on one of the other choices shows the predicted weather.

If the temperature changes significantly as the user moves through the time periods, then the clothing on the avatar changes accordingly. The curved arrows above the clock take the user back to the previous screen. At the bottom of the screen, shown in figure 3.3, are four icons that serve as links to different areas. The icon showing the house is the home screen.

The next icon takes to the viewer to the "Wear?" area. Changes can be made in the weather by tapping on one of eight selections at the top of the page. There is also a scroll bar on the left that allows the user to increase or decrease the temperature. As on the homepage, the avatar's clothing adjusts according to the weather and the temperature. For example, if the student taps on the umbrella icon, the avatar is standing in a puddle, with boots and a raincoat.

The light bulb icon, titled *Trivia,* brings up a screen providing links to the following fourteen areas:

- Fahrenheit to Celsius (converter)
- Animal Weather—Traditional beliefs about how animals can serve as weather predictors
- Clouds—Descriptions of clouds and interesting related theories

Figure 3.3. Homepage of Kid Wether.
Image created by the author.

- Expressions or Idioms—Mostly humorous
- Extreme Weather—Names of storms and record breaking facts
- Instruments—Sixteen instruments with related facts
- Lightning—Related facts, including Ben Franklin's dangerous experiment
- Nursery Rhymes and Song Lyrics
- Rainbow and Sky Colors
- Seasons—What causes seasons, as well as related information
- Top US Snow Cities—Nearly four dozens cities
- US State Records
- Weather Folklore
- Weather Map

That is a large amount of information that teachers can use to teach young students about the weather, the terminology, and the trends. The final icon on the bottom menu bar is a graph where a student can record daily information about the weather. By tapping on eight different weather choices, a student can create a bar chart that shows the weather over a seven-day period.

—⁓—

Leafsnap for iPad
Recommended Grade Levels: 3–10
Developer: Columbia University, University of Maryland, and Smithsonian
    Institution
Website: leafsnap.com/
Cost: Free

Nearly everyone fondly remembers putting together a leaf collection in elementary school. This app was designed as a leaf identification field guide, encouraging students and their parents to get outside and learn about both leaves and trees. Teachers can use the information for class instruction, but they can also assign it as homework. This app is more than just a textbook for leaf identification. It has an amazing built-in *Snap it* feature that allows for identification of collected leaves with just the tap of a finger!

With the quantity of the provided information, this app is appropriate for the high school classroom as well as the elementary grades. The opening screen, which also serves as the home screen, shows the user a slideshow of the collection of 2,590 high-resolution images provided with this app.

Tapping *Browse* on the bottom menu bar brings up details as shown in figure 3.4. The left menu bar includes a listing of 184 tree species. Currently

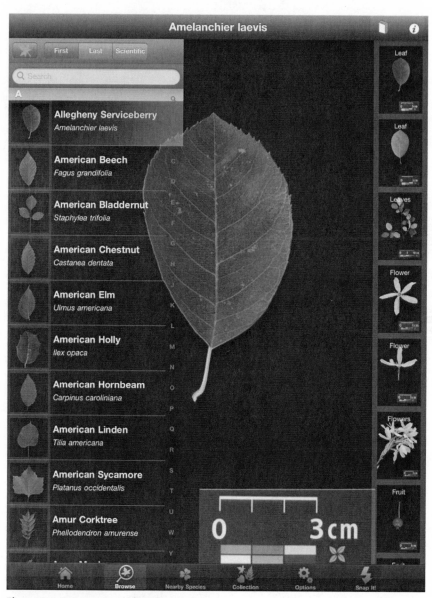

Figure 3.4. Browse Area of Leafsnap.
Image created by the author.

species are primarily from the northeast, but reportedly the designers plan to add species from across the country. When the user selects specific specie on the left, the right menu changes to show different thumbnail views of the associated leaves, flowers, fruits, and bark. Tapping on any of the thumbnail images brings up the full-screen image. Tap on the image itself once to close the left menu and tap again to close the right menu. The scale at the bottom of each image provides the accurate size.

A student can use the search area above the left menu to search for a specific leaf. For example, with a search for *Dogwood,* two choices are provided: the Flowering Dogwood or Kousa Dogwood. The student can tap on the book icon on the top menu to read a paragraph about the tree chosen, including its habitat, growth habit, bloom time, and longevity. Below the description, a map shows the states where this tree can be found.

Below the map are two selections. *Description* is the default, which shows the paragraph description on the top half of the school, but that can be changed to *EOL,* which stands for the *Encyclopedia of Life,* a website with a great deal of details about trees. The website is placed above the map, replacing the paragraph descriptions.

The *Snap It* button on the bottom menu allows students to take pictures of collected leaves. With this amazing feature, from which the app derives its name, the app "snaps" to the corners of the leaf and then provides possible matches. The following two videos help explain this and other features offered with this app:

Introducing LeafSnap—www.youtube.com/watch?v=KCpR4JTEy4c
LeafSnap (Week 3)—www.youtube.com/watch?v=22LdjAeCGpg

—⁓—

Additional High-Rated Science App for the Elementary Classroom
- *Explore the Animal Kingdom Free* by Mathieu Brassard, Free or $1.99— This app contains twenty-eight beautiful pictures of animals with associated names and sounds. It is not included in the main list solely because of the lack of any associated information about the animals.

Science Apps for
Middle School Students (5–8)

Geo Walk HD—3D World Fact Book
Recommended Grade Levels: 6–8
Developer: Vito Technology, Inc.

Website: vitotechnology.com/geowalk.html
Cost: $2.99

Geo Walk provides over 580 pictures in three main categories: *Places, Flora and Fauna,* and *People.* The price was increased in the summer of 2013 from $0.99. However, with the quantity of information, science educators may well deem this app to be worth the investment. Because this is the science chapter, the focus here is only on the *Flora and Fauna* section. However, the *Places* and *People* areas make this app equally valuable for social studies teachers.

When the app is first opened, a globe resting on the back of four elephants appears. When tapped, those elephants move. Spinning the globe brings up little pictures that hover over various areas of the world. Tapping on one of the pictures brings up a view similar to that shown in figure 3.5. Tap on the picture again to see two or three sentences explaining the item in the picture.

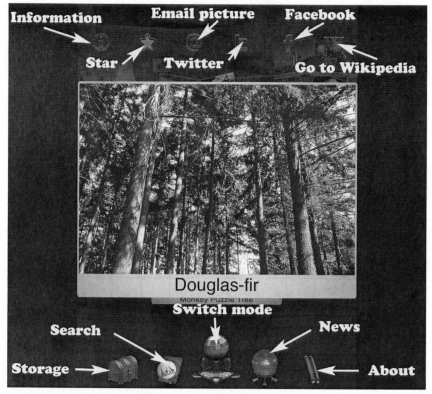

Figure 3.5.   One of over 500 Images Included in GeoWalk.
Image created by the author.

Above and below the image are eleven links that offer a variety of options. Tapping on the *Information* button at the top left flips the slide to an information area; tap on the button again to return to the image. The *Star* saves the picture as one of a user's favorites. Whenever a favorite is selected, a miniature of the picture shows in the background, providing a shortcut to the picture. Tap on it to open it at any time. The @ symbol on the top menu bar allows the user to e-mail the picture to whomever he or she wishes. Students can e-mail it to their teacher, to themselves, or to a collaborative group.

Similarly, a picture can be sent to Twitter or Facebook by tapping on one of the next two buttons. The last button on the top menu brings up a Wikipedia page that gives full information about the picture. Tapping on the little graphic of a treasure chest opens what appears to be an old document with the categories of *Places, Animals, Plants, People,* and *Events.* Initially all the areas are selected. However, a science teacher might want to limit the selection of pictures by only choosing one or two of the areas.

Tapping on the second icon on the bottom menu brings up a searchable list of all images included with this app in alphabetical order by first name. For example, when searching for Darwin, a student would need to know that his first name was Charles. However, there is a search area at the very top of that list. Typing in just "Darwin" takes the user to "Charles Robert Darwin."

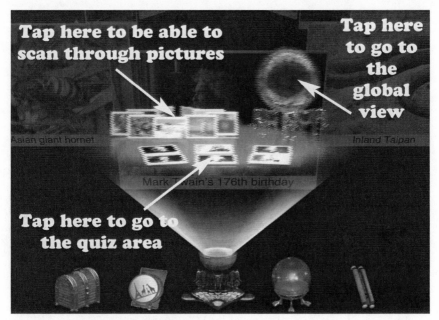

Figure 3.6.   Options for GeoWalk.
Image created by the author.

The middle icon in the bottom menu bar offers a selection from three areas, as shown in figure 3.6. Tapping in the lower area brings up a quiz. Questions are posed at the top.

The topics covered by these questions relate to what was selected while using the treasure chest icon. With each question, images appear below, one of which represents the correct answer. When an answer is chosen a card shows information about the selection. If the answer is correct, the name of the picture is underlined in green.

Tap anywhere to bring up the next question. If an incorrect answer is chosen, the name is underlined in red and the same question remains until the correct picture is selected. The other two areas to view are either the global view or the scrollable pictures view. The fourth icon on the bottom menu brings up news events. The last icon on the right simply brings up information about Vito Technology, Inc.

—⟪ϕϕ⟫—

Science 360 for iPad
Recommended Grade Levels: 5–12
Developer: National Science Foundation
Website: science360.gov/ipad/, science360.gov/files/
Cost: Free (also available on Android)

With this app, the National Science Foundation provides a extensive collection of awesome images and videos, all related to a branch of science. The collection was gathered from scientists and colleges and universities from around the world. A recent *PC Magazine* described the collection as being "sure to intrigue and delight even the most science-phobic among us" (Hoffman, 2012). As the app first loads, only an array of the site's logo are viewable. However, the logos gradually transform to a matrix of thumbnails of the hundreds of images and videos.

A two-finger spread brings a closer view, with a brief description with each thumbnail image. The name *360* comes from the fact that users can scroll in any direction through twelve rows and eighteen columns that then begin to repeat as if they were wrapped around a 360-degree globe. Scrolling may be tedious, especially when searching for a previously viewed video. The easiest way to search through this collection is to start by tapping the screen with a single two-finger tap, which brings up a menu with links to four areas: *saved, tags, news,* and *more.*

Tapping on *tags* takes the user to an alphabetical listing of all the tags associated with each of the videos in this collection. If a physics teacher, for

TITLE: The world of birds
BC: 32091045661700
DUE: 10-31-14

TITLE: Not a toy, but a tool : an educat
BC: 32091045227718
DUE: 10-31-14

TITLE: The deuce and a half iPad : an ed
BC: 32091045227775
DUE: 10-31-14

TITLE: Cruise Alaska [videorecording]
BC: 32091032194731
DUE: 10-17-14

TITLE: Alaska's Inside Passage [videorec
BC: 32091035142950
DUE: 10-17-14

You can't put a price on friendship...
but how does $5 sound? Join The Friends.

example, wanted to search for a video of Newton's Three Laws of Motion, she or he would simply tap on *N* at the top menu and then scroll down the N column. There is a video titled "Newton's Laws of Motion," with a subtitle "Science of NHL Hockey."

The teacher can also tap on the small magnifying glass at the top right of the *tags* screen, which allows "Newton" or any other query to be typed. Typing "Newton" there brings up videos that discuss the laws of motion, even though "Newton" is not in the title. During video playback, a collection of links is available; a description of the function of each is added in figure 3.7.

If the user taps on the star during video playback, the star turns blue and the video is then kept in the *Favorites* section. The two-finger tap brings up the same four-item menu mentioned in the previous paragraph. Tapping on the *Star* at the top takes the user to the page that shows all the videos selected as favorites. Below the *Star* on that menu, is the *News* area where there is a list of more than a dozen recent news items that relate to science, each with its associated video. These images and videos have tremendous value by

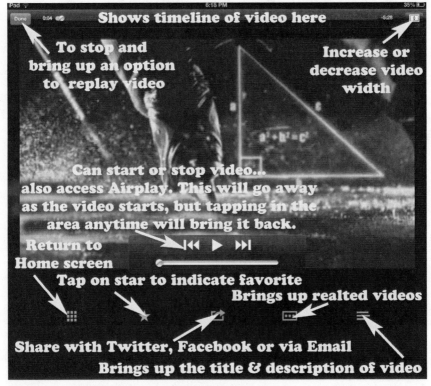

Figure 3.7. Links Available during the Playing of a Video.
Image created by the author.

engaging middle or high school science students and helping them to acquire a fuller understanding of important scientific concepts.

—~*@*~—

Build a Body
Recommended Grade Levels: 6–8
Developer: Spongelab Interactive
Website: www.spongelab.com/game_pages/BAB_ios.cfm#1
Cost: Free

The goal of this app, as the name indicates, is to build a body as quickly as possible. The opening screen provides three options: *Start, Help/Info,* and *Leaderboard.* The *Help/Info* area is a good place to start. The information there is exactly the same as is shown on the website. One of those directions comments that "Build-a-body is an awesome tool to introduce and teach concepts of human anatomy and human physiology."

The app is very intuitive, requiring a student to drag organs and bones to the appropriate area of a skeleton in as short as time as possible. This game does require that the user has studied some prior to trying to move parts in

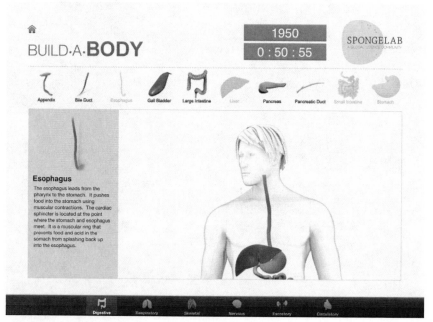

Figure 3.8.   Skeletal System in Build-a-Body.
Image created by the author.

the correct position. As the player drags each organ or bone down, a statement about the function is shown, which sometimes provides a clue concerning the correct position. Figure 3.8 shows that only the stomach, small intestines, liver, and esophagus have been placed in the correct position. Six other parts of the digestive system are waiting to be moved.

The esophagus was the last to be moved, so the information about that organ is showing on the left side. The time shows that the user started the game almost fifty-one seconds earlier. Altogether there are six different areas:

- Digestive
- Respiratory
- Skeletal
- Nervous
- Excretory
- Circulatory

—〰—

EMD PTE
Recommended Grade Levels: 7–10
Developer: EMD Chemicals
Website: www.emdmillipore.com/chemicals/iphone-and-ipad-app-interactive
-periodic-table/c_9Seb.s1OvkMAAAEvu8ZQnwIC
Cost: Free (also available on Android)

The name of this app does not explain much about its focus. However, on the EMD logo, the words *Periodic Table* indicate the true function. This app is an interactive periodic table. The website listed previously describes the app as "simple, concise and intuitive" with "well-arranged groups and periods, [and] detailed pages for every element." The table uses ten colors to differentiate the classifications of the 112 elements.

Tap on any element and a small window comes up to show the element's designation, classification, group, period, and relative atomic mass. Tap on that window and it rotates to provide considerably more information, divided into five categories:

- General
- Basic Information
- Discoverer
- Picture Element
- Products for Analytical Testing

The *Basic Information* section provides details that would be more appropriate for high school or university level chemistry. Yet there is even more! In the upper left area of the main screen resides a little M. Tapping on that M brings out a menu bar with the following eight items:

- Search
- Classification
- Atomic Properties
- State at Room Temperature
- Property Ranking
- Discovery
- Molar Mass Calculator
- Glossary

A user can also access that menu by simply holding the iPad with the left side up. The menu appears to slide out of a slot. Hold the left side down and the menu slides back into its slot. Tapping on the top item, *Search*, brings up a list of all the elements, sorted alphabetically by the symbols. At the top, a search area is also provided, for typing in the element's name or symbol.

The glossary area contains over sixty terms that all relate to chemistry. Especially considering that this is currently a free app, it should be considered essential for any teacher or student of chemistry. Some information may be more appropriate for high school. However, the intuitive approach of this app makes a great way to introduce young scholars to the field of chemistry.

—◦◦◦—

Rocket Science 101
Recommended Grade Levels: 7–10
Developer: NASA
Website: www.nasa.gov/externalflash/RocketScience101/RocketScience101 .html
Cost: Free (also available on Android)

Rockets are very popular with students. For that reason, this app can really spark student interest. NASA has always been great at sharing quality information and resources that are free. This app is no exception. The home screen shows three levels of participation: *Have Fun, Challenge Yourself,* and *Rocket Scientist.* Even the *Have Fun* level provides basic information about how to build a basic rocket and the importance of the various stages.

If a student chooses *Challenge Yourself,* the next screen requires that the student select one of eight missions. The eight choices are all rockets that have actually been launched for a variety of missions. Before making a final selection, a student can tap on a selection, read the information about the mission, and then scroll through the other missions to learn an overview of each one.

After reading all the summaries, a student can then make an informed decision. If the GOES-O mission is selected, the student then is asked to select one of four rockets. Only one rocket is the correct choice. Explanations are given if the student selects the wrong rocket. Next the student needs to assemble the six parts of the rocket into their correct position. As soon as the green *Launch* button is pressed, the screen shows a simulation of the actual launch. Throughout the flight of the rocket, the various stages are explained.

In the *Rocket Scientist* section, a selection from the same eight rocket missions must be made. This time, there are fifteen different rocket parts, rather than the six from the *Challenge Yourself* section. Figure 3.9 shows the rocket about half way through the building stage. Additional comments have been added to figure 3.9 to further explain the various features. This is a fantastic app, especially considering the price. It is clearly appropriate for both middle school and high school classrooms. The National Association of Rocketry (NAR) website (www.nar.org/teacher.html) provides additional resources for NAR teachers and youth group leaders.

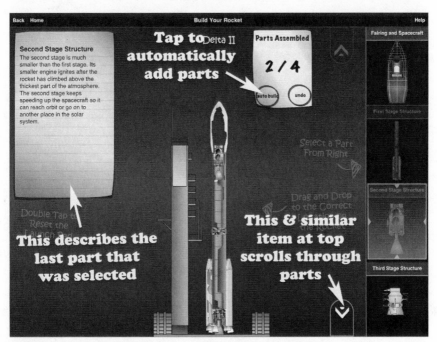

Figure 3.9.   Rocket Scientist Section, with Comments Added.
Image created by the author.

Science Apps for High School Students (9–12)

A typical high school might offer as many as six or seven courses under the umbrella of science. That is, in addition to the four major subjects of physical science, biology, chemistry, and physics, there are subjects like botany, earth science, astronomy, and ecology, as well as a selection of AP subjects. In addition to the problem of having so many subjects to cover, the pool of quality science apps frankly is quite extensive.

This text covers one app for each of the following four subjects:

- Physical science
- Biology
- Chemistry
- Physics

In addition, an app is included that focuses on allowing students to address key science-related issues. However, readers who are interested in science should take advantage of the list of additional apps at the end of this chapter.

—⚡—

PhysicalSci
Recommended Grade Levels: 7–10
Developer: CPO Science
Website: None currently available for this app.
Cost: Free

The home screen bears the title *Physical Science: Interactive Glossary*. The app covers six major categories of science:

- Energy and Systems
- Force and Motion
- Electricity and Magnetism
- Matter and Energy
- Light and Optics
- Sound and Waves

Enough material is included in this app to supplement topics for an entire year of study, either in physical science or physics. The app approaches each topic either with a section of videos and animations called the *Master Glossary* section, or with a section of *Flash Cards*. In the effort to select apps that make science both fun and "funny," this app was chosen because of the glossary, not the flash cards.

As an example, first tap on the *Electricity and Magnetism* graphic on the homepage. On the left side of the screen are the subtopics, which in this case include fifteen different subtopics. Tapping on *Parallel Circuit* brings up an animated video ready to play. Not all videos are animations. Many have instructors talking about topics with a related demonstration. Altogether the app contains a total of ninety-seven subtopics. With each subtopic, there are usually related videos. Figure 3.10 shows the menu for the *Electricity and Magnetism* area. *Electric Current* is the subtopic selected with one *Featured Simulation* video, as well as two other videos in the *Related Content* area.

This app also has available *Flash Cards* composed of definitions of all the major terms within each category. In figure 3.10, there is a link to the *Flash Cards* section in the upper right corner. The cards can be viewed in alphabetical order or there is a shuffle button to randomize the order. Especially considering the price, the videos make this another "must have" app for any science teacher or student. The videos can easily be projected, even if only one iPad is available in the classroom.

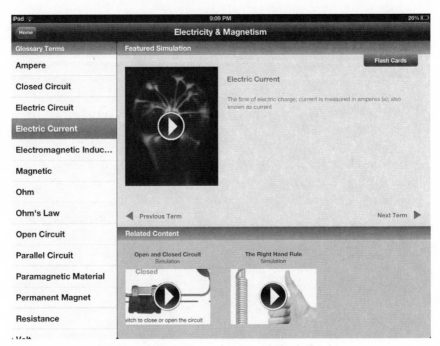

Figure 3.10. Electricity and Magnetism Selections of Physical Sci.
Image created by the author.

—◦◦◦—

Power of Minus Ten (POMT)—Cells and Genetics
Recommended Grade Levels: 7–12
Developer: Green-Eye Visualization
Website: powersofminusten.com/
Cost: $1.99 (also available on Android through Dynamoid Apps)

The inspiration for this app stems from a documentary short film, *Powers of Ten*, made in 1968 by Ray and Charles Eames. That film begins with a view of space facing an invisible earth from a distance of many light years away (10^{24} meters). Zooming in begins, eventually bringing the solar system into view, and then the earth. The film continues zooming in to the North American continent, then to the United States, then to Chicago, and then to a person lying on a blanket by Lake Michigan. The journey continues zooming in to the skin level into the person's hand to show microscopic levels of magnification (10^{-16} meters).

This app only focuses on the range from skin level to the subatomic level. Unlike the film, this app is interactive and includes instructional information that was not possible when the documentary was originally made. The opening screen has a link to type the name of the user. There is also a settings link for turning off the sound and some other features, if desired. When the *Play* button is tapped, a human hand appears on the next screen.

There are also instructions for zooming in, either by a two-finger spread or by using the scale on the left side of the screen. Figure 3.11 shows the human skin at the cellular (30-μm) level. The user earns points in this "game" by tapping on the various structures shown in each screen. As a cell or molecule is tapped, an information box appears. In figure 3.11, the white arrow has been added to show the last point that was tapped, which brings up the scrollable box about the metaphase of mitosis.

Tapping on the *LAB* button on the upper right accesses an area that provides lists of all the terms and phases with associated explanations. Game challenges can also be set up. This app explores worlds down to the molecular level (3×10^{-10} m) and has won many awards, as documented on the website. Biology teachers should also go to the App Store and load the equally engaging free app *Power of Minus Ten—Bones*. Students are bound to enjoy using both these apps to learn key biological topics.

The Powers of Ten documentary—www.cosmolearning.com/documentaries/powers-of-ten-1583/1/

Figure 3.11. Cellular Level of Human Skin.
Image created by the author.

——~~—

Chem Pro: Chemistry Tutor
Recommended Grade Levels: 9–12
Developer: iHelpNYC
Website: www.ihelpnyc.com/
Cost: Free or $4.99 (also available on Android)

Chemistry is not an easy subject for many high school students. This app is ideal for reinforcing topics already taught in the classroom. The free version only includes ten topics, whereas the $4.99 version includes a total of eighty topics. The following list shows the ten topics that come with the free version, along with the length of the associated video:

1. Intro to Chemistry—with 8 min. 26 sec. video lesson
2. Atomic Mass—with 15 min. 45 sec. video lesson
3. Ionic Compounds—with 15 min. 34 sec. video lesson
4. Moles—with 24 min. 5 sec. video lesson
5. Elemental Analysis—with 19 min. 7 sec. video lesson

6. Balancing Reactions—with 12 min. 37 sec. video lesson
7. Stoichiometry—with 25 min. 39 sec. video lesson
8. Limiting Reagents—with 30 min. 3 sec. video lesson
9. Molarity—with 19 min. 52 sec. video lesson
10. Solution Reactions—with 22 min. 51 sec. video lesson

The topics are listed on a left menu bar. An overview of the lesson with the time needed to play the video is always in the lower right area. The video itself is shown in the upper right section of the screen, but can be played at full screen. The bottom menu has five links. The *Lessons* section, which is where the videos are seen, serves as the default setting. The videos are not flashy, but include basic summaries of key topics.

The *Flash Cards* section is the next icon on the bottom menu, which brings up nine different areas. Only the set for *Common Element Names* are available at no extra expense. Each of the other sets is available for purchase at $0.99 each. Although I tend to steer away from flash cards, they are certainly justified here because recognizing the symbols for the various elements is an essential part of learning this subject.

The *Tools* icon brings up the interactive periodic table. A student can tap on the symbol of any element, such as *Fe*, to show in the top area the element's name, atomic number, and atomic weight. The *Tools* area is also where a student can access either the *Molar Mass Calculator* or the *Unit Converter*. Purchased alone, the *Unit Converter* needs a fee of $0.99, but it is included in the $4.99 version, with no additional fee.

Tapping the fourth icon, the *Equation Sheet*, brings up a five-page sheet that has over seventy scientific equations. Then the final area, *Contact*, simply provides information about the designer. The various features in this app go a long way in covering many of the key topics in any high school general chemistry course.

—*ww*—

Exploriments: Newton's Law of Universal Gravitation
Recommended Grade Levels: 9–12
Developer: Exploriments.com
Website: www.exploriments.com/ipad/Gravitation.html
Cost: $1.99

Finding a physics app that stands out above all others presented a decided challenge, primarily because physics covers such a broad range of topics. Topics including mechanics, work and energy, electricity and magnetism, light, sound, waves, thermodynamics, the structure and behavior of atoms, and more are all within the realm of physics. So the search focused on finding an app from one of those areas that would ignite a sense of excitement in students, without being priced beyond the $1.99 limit set for this book.

Several excellent apps rose to the top. *Exploriments* was selected, but several others are in the *Additional Valuable Apps* listing at the end of the chapter. *Exploriments* covers five instructional activities that all relate to Newton's Law of Gravitation. Gravity is a very important concept for high school students to understand. Yet how various masses behave because of gravity is far more complex than just knowing that "what goes up must come down." This app goes a long way toward showing students the relationship between gravity, mass, distance, and weight.

The five topics in the *Activities* area of the app are listed here:

1. Exploring Newton's Law of Universal Gravitation
2. Firing Newton's Orbital Cannon
3. Putting a Satellite into Orbit
4. Studying the Effect of Altitude on "g"
5. Deducing the Radius and Mass of a Planet by Varying the Altitude of a Satellite

Each activity is interactive. A student should be allowed to work with this app individually if at all possible. Teachers can provide guidelines and then require a report on specific observations and conclusions that the student may have drawn. For the first activity, a student can watch the effect of increasing the masses of the two objects, as well as varying the distances. This animation is great for showing how the force of gravity is affected by a change in one variable. In addition, the *Guide* button at the top right offers several different informational areas.

Figure 3.12 shows an activity that is always of great interest to the students. The animation shows Newton's Orbital Cannon thought experiment. Newton used the following question to explain the principle of orbits: "How fast would a cannon ball need to be shot to achieve orbit around the earth?" Figure 3.12 shows the paths of five successive launches of the cannon ball, each at a different initial velocities.

The fourth attempt allowed the cannon to achieve orbital velocity at a low attitude. The last attempt is shown in progress. The cannon ball is approaching the completion of its first orbit at the maximum speed at which the cannon would retain orbit. The launch speed is always shown at the lower left.

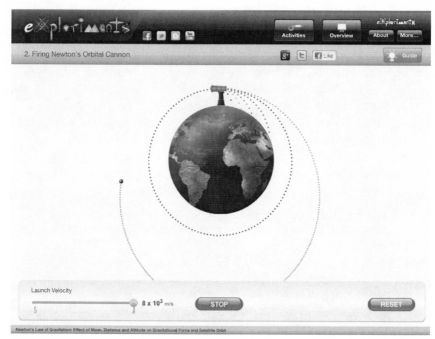

Figure 3.12. Firing Newton's Orbital Cannon.
Image created by the author.

The top of figure 3.12 shows a collection of links seen with every activity. The *Overview* button opens a window with a short summary of the activity. The *Guide* offers areas to *Map*, *Explore*, and *Discover*, each with more detailed information. The *More* button shows that there are fourteen more *Exploriments* apps that all relate to an area of physics. A great deal of learning can be achieved through the use of all the *Exploriments* apps. Further information is included in the *Additional Highly Rated Apps* near the end of this chapter.

———❧———

NASA Science: A Journey of Discovery
Recommended Grade Levels: 7–12
Developer: NASA
Website: science.nasa.gov/connect/apps/
Cost: Free

As mentioned earlier in this chapter, NASA has always had a willingness to share quality material with educators. This app focuses on information learned from various NASA missions. Teachers can use this not only for instruction, but also for discussions concerning how to respond to four major questions. Each of the following topics are engaging and would be valuable to address in most any science classroom:

1. What are the effects of space weather on Earth's technology?
2. How are Earth's sea, ice, and ice sheets changing?
3. Are there other habitable planets?
4. Was Mars ever a habitat for life?

Each of the four questions appears on the homepage below an image. Tapping on one of those images brings up a small window with some details about an answer. The first question about the effects of space weather on Earth's technology brings the user to a screen with links to nine different space events, such as the solar cycle, solar flares, geomagnetic storms, and asteroids and comets.

When entering the area about the earth's ice and ice sheets changing, the first window shows all the continents with key area tags. On the top menu are the five links, covering the following topics:

- Causes
- Ice Sheets
- Sea Ice
- Sea Level
- Glossary

Figure 3.13 shows the screen that comes up when the student taps on *Causes*. Also three other informative areas can be opened; one is a video about the increase in carbon dioxide concentrations around the world.

On the main screens, in addition to the five areas accessible from the top menu, three links on the bottom menu take the user to informational areas about three different NASA missions that recently have studied the issues covered in this app: The Ice, Cloud, and Land Elevation Satellite (ICESat), the Gravity Recovery and Climate Experiment (GRACE), and the IceBridge mission.

Magnificent NASA images are available throughout this app. A great deal of science can be learned through the study of the app's four main questions. Discussing scientific issues like these is a valuable activity. Teachers can help students realize that understanding science is an important part of becoming an informed citizen in the twenty-first century.

Figure 3.13. Causes of Changes in Earth's Sea Ice and Ice Sheets.
Image created by the author.

Apps Appropriate for the Science Classroom, but Described Elsewhere

- *Elementary School: Booksy: Learn to Read Platform for K–2* by Tipitap, Inc., Free—This app is discussed in chapter 4 of *Not a Toy, but a Tool*. In addition to *The Humpback Whale*, several of the $0.99 books are appropriate for teaching science to young children. Learning the sounds that animals make is a popular activity with children.
- *Elementary & Middle School: Mathmateer* by Dan Russell-Pinson, Free or $0.99—This app is discussed in chapter 2 of this book. This app is also great for science class. Students can be taught about balance, thrust, angle of inclination, and other topics. Awards can be given for students who achieve the highest altitude.
- *High School: PrepZilla Study with Friends Game* by gWhiz, LLC, Free— This app is discussed in chapter 2 of this book. Topics include AP chemistry, AP physics, AP environmental science, and Regents Exam: Biology

Additional Highly Rated Apps for High School Science

This section lists additional apps for high school science. Each has features that can help teachers promote student learning in various areas of science.

Biology
1. *Molecules* by Sunset Lake Software, Free—This is a highly rated app that shows three-dimensional views of six molecules, each with associated information.
2. *Virtual Cell Animations* by VCell Productions, Free—With videos, graphics, and quizzes, this app covers cellular respiration, protein expression, and RNA expression. Terms may be a bit advanced for the high school level.
3. *3D Brain* by Cold Spring Harbor Laboratory, Free—This excellent, highly rated app is relevant for both high school– and college-level biology.
4. *Frog Dissection* by Emantras, Inc., $3.99—This is a truly excellent app, but the price prevented it from being more fully covered in this book.

Chemistry
1. *Science House* by Object Enterprises, Free—This is an awesome app with a couple of annoying features. The awesome part is that it contains eighty chemistry-related videos, showing demonstrations on a broad range of topics. This is perfect for showing in high school classrooms! However, this app has a low rating for two reason: (1) at the end of each video, the user must quit the app altogether, then reopen in order to play another video; and (2) each video took awhile to load before being ready to play.
2. *NOVA Elements* by PBS, Free—A must-have app for any chemistry teacher, this app includes three main areas: (1) WATCH: videos from PBS's Hunting the Elements show, (2) EXPLORE: an interactive periodic table, and (3) PLAY: a game that takes the user to a "molecular sandbox" where students can build atoms and molecules. This is an incredible fun area in which students can learn details about the structure of atoms and molecules.

Physics
1. *iBlackbody* by Georgia Tech, $0.99—briefly mentioned in chapter 1 of this book.
2. *Vernier Video Physics* by Vernier Software & Technology, $4.99—The Vernier company was started in the early 1980s by David Vernier, a high school physics teacher. The company first produced excellent science software for Apple II computers on large large floppy disks. Their expertise with quality educational programs has continued. These videos are superior and well worth the price.

3. *SimPhysics* by SimInsights, Inc., Free—This is an excellent app. Some may be bothered by the requirement to log in through Facebook. Regardless, there are valuable exercises, covering thirty-eight physics-related topics.
4. *Ohmulator* by David Caddy, $0.99—This app is outstanding for showing the relationships between voltage, current, and resistance.
5. *Physics 2 HD* by Hanz Meyer, Free—This app is for reference, not for instruction. This app provides over seventy pages of formulas, definitions, and explanations all related to physics. Students can certainly use this as an excellent reference tool for physics.
6. In addition to the *Exploriments* app mentioned in this chapter, the designer has created additional *Exploriments* apps, all high quality and varying in price from free to $2.99. The topics cover motion (six apps), fluids (one app), electrostatics (one app), electricity (four apps), force (three apps), and light (one app). For more information, readers can go to the following site and click on the tab that is associated with each of those topics: www.exploriments.com/ipad/index.html.

Reflections of Chapter Three

Altogether forty-six different apps have been addressed in this chapter, either with full discussions or by being included in a list of additional valuable apps. Each of these apps has the ability to encourage fun and discovery in the science classroom.

Author Isaac Asimov had a tremendous influence on popularizing science through his prolific writing of science fiction stories and books. Today the iPad can have a similarly strong influence on how students view the study of science. Through the use of apps, students begin to be fascinated by this awesome field of study, in which every topic can bring intrigue and surprise.

CHAPTER FOUR

Teaching Art and Music
with the iPad

The recent trend of many school districts to cut art and music from their school curriculum is quite disturbing. Tragically, for many school systems across our country, a combination of the lack of funds and the demands of the No Child Left Behind Act have sounded the death knell for art and music programs. I have always felt blessed by attending K–12 schools that valued both these subjects.

Growing up in Philadelphia brought further blessings of attending the concerts of the renowned Philadelphia Orchestra, which, at the time, was under the direction of Eugene Ormandy, one of the world's best-known conductors. Also, having a student membership at the Philadelphia Art Museum was equally delightful. This is one of the most beautiful museums in the world, both inside and out. They provide outstanding workshops and tours.

However, students in more rural areas are not blessed with an ability to sit in a symphony hall surrounded by the beauty of classical music. Visiting a large art museum filled with treasures from times past is another experience denied to those who live a good distance from major cities.

Recently, a teacher from the Appalachian area of east Tennessee was giving a ride home to a fourteen-year-old girl. The car radio was on a classical music station. The teenager asked, "What kind of music is this?" Their school system has not had music in the curriculum for several years. Stories like that are playing out across our nation. An appreciation of the arts is being lost to an entire generation.

Sir Ken Robinson (TEDx Talks Director, 2007), who is referenced in chapter 1 of this book, believes that "the arts should be on an equal footing in schools with the sciences, humanities, languages and physical education." Art and music should not be considered a luxury, but rather a necessity. In the fall of 2009, a committee of The College Board conducted a research study titled *Arts at the Core*. The study found that students who take four years of arts and music classes while in high school score 91 points better on their SAT exams than students who took only a half-year or less.

Specifically, scores averaged 1070 among students who had received ample arts education, compared with 979 for students who were denied those courses. The apps covered in this chapter are valuable tools for enhancing existing arts programs. If the music and art classes are minimal or nonexistent, parents and teachers of other subjects should be proactive by using these apps to strengthen student knowledge of both those areas.

This chapter includes an equal number of music app and art apps, although they are not equally distributed amongst grade levels. The elementary level weighs in a bit more heavily on the art apps, whereas the high school level has more music apps. Also, near the end of the chapter, there is a large collection of *Additional Valuable Apps* covering a range of subjects in the arts.

Art and Music Apps for
Elementary School Students (K–4)

Doodle Monkey—Free Draw & Sketch
Recommended Grade Levels: PK–2
Developer: BakedSoft
Website: none available for app; design's webpage: help.bakedsoft.com/
Cost: Free

The simplicity of this app makes it perfect for young children. After a brief opening screen, the drawing area opens, which covers the vast majority of the screen. Nine basics colors are available on the left of the lower menu bar. As each color is selected, a small shadow of a hand covers the color to indicate the current selection. To the right of the color choices, three tools are available: a pencil, a pen, and a paintbrush. The pen is the default selection. The difference between the three tools is simply the width of the stroke. The pencil creates a very narrow line and the paintbrush has the widest stroke. To the right of the tools is the eraser tool and then the *undo* and *redo* buttons, which both allow for repeated steps.

Figure 4.1. Drawing Area of Doodle Monkey.
Image created by the author.

The top menu provides three links. The dropdown menu from the top left offers links to areas with information about the designer. In the right corner, the red heart saves the image to the Photo area of the iPad. Once saved, the image can then be e-mailed to a teacher. The small image to the left of the heart provides access to the iPad's Camera Roll and all created Albums. Users can select a picture and then draw on it with the same tools that were available to the blank screen. Without a doubt, this is a great app for encouraging creativity.

⟶✦✦✦⟵

Art of Glow
Recommended Grade Levels: 1–6
Developer: Natenai Ariyatrakool
Website: www.natenai.com/iphone/art_of_glow/
Cost: Free or $0.99 (also available on Android)

Art of Glow is a must-have for the creative student. The menus can be hard to understand for the youngest students, but they still enjoy using it. A paid version rids the screen the any advertisements and also allows the creations of the young artist to be saved. Of course, with the free app, the user can take a screen snapshot, but the border advertisement would also show. Being able to save the videos of the creations is definitely worth the investment.

The *Tools* icon is a circle with a small wrench and hammer, located in the lower right corner. After tapping on that icon, the menu pops up to offer several options for setting up the image, such as the shape, the size, the life time (duration), et cetera. In addition to the features shown, the user can tap next to *Shape* to bring up a new menu with eight different shapes. On that new menu, rather than choosing a specific color, the user can choose to *CYCLE* through the colors; to *RANDOM EACH FINGER*, which means that a different color is selected randomly with each finger tap; or *FULL RANDOM*, which allow the colors to change randomly.

Any image can be saved by first tapping on the *Tools* icon and then the *Video* tab just to the right of the *Tools* tab. Then tap on the *Save Image* button. A pop-up message appears notifying the user that the image has been saved to the Photo Album. That is the preferred method to save images, as the tools icon is then not visible in the image. If a user takes a snapshot of the image, the tools icon would be visible.

Tapping on the *Camera* tab brings up the menu, which allows the user to select from several pre-made images. This menu also allows users to save videos. The *Welcome Demo* runs through several samples of basic premade videos. After tapping on the *Clear* button and then selecting *Record New*, every step taken in the process of making a new creation is recorded.

When finished with the creation, the user should tap on the *Tools* icon and then the *Video* tab. When the *Stop Recording* button is tapped, the user can type in a name for the creation and then finish by tapping *OK* and *Done*. The creation can be replayed at any time by tapping on the *Video* tab and then selecting the name of the creation, listed below the *Welcome Demo*.

—⁓—

ColorMixer HD
Recommended Grade Levels: 1–4
Developer: Ricardo R da Silva
Website: www.rrdas.org/games/colormixer-hd.html
Cost: $0.99; $0.99 for each package of additional coloring page sets

ColorMixer is an excellent app for teaching young artists the effects of mixing primary colors to achieve a vast array of different colors. The opening screen, which offers three options for purchasing more coloring pages, can

Figure 4.2. Partially Completed Drawing in Color Mixer HD.
Image created by the author.

be bypassed as desired. The next screen allows the user to select one of forty coloring pages. Figure 4.2 shows a partially completed image.

At first, the more than two dozen menu items may seem a bit intimidating for young children. However, the function of each feature easily can be learned by tapping on the *question mark,* which is the third icon from the right on the lower menu. Tapping there brings up the image of a dog with the message, "Just tap an item to see the explanation or tap the button with an 'x' near me to dismiss me." After that, as a feature is tapped, a pop-up message explains how to use the selected feature.

Art teachers especially appreciate the feature of the cup where various quantities of the primary colors are combined to create other colors. For example, if a color green is needed, the teacher can explain to students that they can start by placing yellow into the empty cup. Then the blue paint is slowly added. At first, there is minimal effect, but gradually the cup first turns very light green and then a dark green.

Teachers should also explain that, throughout the mixing process, students should watch the image in the lower left corner of a screen, which always shows the percentage composition of the primary colors. When starting with yellow, the middle bar is entirely yellow. After blue is selected and gradually added to the cup, the blue bar gains height. When the cup is clearly green, the blue bar is still only half the height of the yellow bar. Eventually, if the user continues to tap, the cup begins to turn fully blue, as the yellow bar loses color.

Another important area is the top left. When the user needs to fill a very small area on the main screen, the area in the upper left provides a crosshair that indicates the exact area about to be filled. The user's finger can move the crosshair, as needed. Pressing hard then fills the selected area.

Website: www.youtube.com/watch?v=FRLaZ5lB6jc

Additional Highly Rated Apps for Elementary Art Classes:
- *Brushes 3* by Taptrix, Inc., Free—Full-screen painting with value for elementary through high school. Lots of features, including being able to record and replay paintings.
- *Puppet Pals HD* by Polished Play, LLC, Free—Students are able to create their own shows with selected characters, backdrop, animation and audio. Encourages fun and creativity!
- *Faces iMake*—Four versions, all by iMagine machine LLC; won the Parents' Choice Gold Award in 2013.
  - *Faces iMake: ABC*, $1.99—Geared for preschool age children.
  - *Faces iMake: Lite*, $0.99—Similar to a digital Mr. Potato Head; best for elementary children.
  - *Faces iMake: Premier*, $1.99—Same as cheaper versions, but with more features.
  - *Faces iMake: Right Brain Creativity*, $4.99—Same as cheaper versions, but, as the expression goes, "on steroids." The app encourages creativity galore!

—◦◦◦—

Notes!—Learn To Read Music
Recommended Grade Levels: 3–4
Developer: Visions Encoded Inc.
Website: visionsencoded.com/fun-iphone-apps/
Cost: $0.99 and $0.99 each for five other similar apps

This app allows a young student who is new to music to learn the names of notes. The first time the app is opened, the graphic of a hand moves to demonstrate the main features. A keyboard is at the bottom of the screen with a note on a staff with the treble clef. Tapping anywhere on the staff rotates the image to reveal a staff with the bass clef.

The challenge is for the student to tap on the key that corresponds to the position of the note shown on the staff above. If an incorrect selection is made, the key that was tapped turns red briefly. If the correct selection is made, the note turns green, a trophy briefly appears, and the sound of that note is heard. Then the note on the staff moves to a new position.

At the center top of the screen are three circles, which control the keyboard appearance. When the middle one is black, each of the keys of the keyboard has a letter written on it that corresponds to the name of the note. Figure 4.3 shows that the circle to the left brings up a keyboard with no letters. As a student becomes more familiar with the letters, this provides the challenge of learning the keys as they appear on a regular keyboard.

The circle on the right brings up just the letters in their proper sequence, but without any keyboard showing at all. This allows students to practice the recognition of the names of notes. Those three circles at the top function the same for both the treble and bass clefs.

Figure 4.3. Notes! Selection at Top Leaves Keys Unlabeled.
Image created by the author.

Tapping on the *Settings* icon in the upper right brings up a screen that allows the user to switch between three note scales: the current standard lettering scale; the German scale, in which Hs replace all Bs; or the Do-Re-Mi-Fa-Sol-La-Si lettering used primarily for vocal purposes. The *i* in the upper left simply takes the user to the webpage. Four links at the bottom take the user to the App store to purchase the other apps available from the designer of this app. An arrow at the top left takes the user back to the main screen.

—~~~—

Little Mozart
Recommended Grade Levels: 3–4
Developer: Imagina
Website: mozart.imagina.pt/
Cost: Free or $3.99

This app provides a superb method for introducing young children to the thrill of composing their own music. A student can select the notes that appear on a staff and then also select various instruments to accompany the little Mozart graphic as he plays the newly created music on his piano. The introductory screen shows a picture of a home and plays the song that includes the lines, "There's a house where music lives."

The front steps of the home are piano keys and the pillars by the front door are flutes. Simply tap on *My Device* to get started. The next screen shows little Mozart with two buttons to each side of him. The button in the lower left corner is for returning to the introductory page. Next is the *Settings* button. The button just to the right of Mozart takes students to the screen where new music can be composed. The final button in the lower right corner provides a link to the saved compositions of the student, as well as twelve presaved "Little Mozart melodies."

Tapping on the *Settings* button brings the user to a screen with six possible selections. The button on the upper left opens up a new window that allows the user to select measure bars, black and white notes, or colored notes. Tap anywhere on the background to return to the six buttons. The top middle button offers three options for *Composition Rules: With All Rules, With No Rules,* and *With Duration Rules.*

The third button on the top row offers two choices for creating a composition with or without help. For a student new to the field of music composition, the help is usually preferable, although it usually comes in the form of audio recordings, so teachers need to consider the value for classroom use.

Earphones, of course, would be valuable to have in this case. The button with the British flag allows users to switch from English to Portuguese, if desired. The button with the musical notes allows the user to mute the background music that plays on some screens. The last button provides a toggle switch for muting the speech on various screens.

The composition area is the most important area of this app. Notes can be added to the staff and instruments can also be selected to accompany Mozart as he plays the piano. The instruments that can be selected for use include the piano, English flute, violin, trumpet, and xylophone. The user can listen to the creation by tapping on the arrow to the right of the staff.

This free app allows for considerable creativity, along with ample instruction on the art of musical composition. For those who want even more, the paid version offers two main advantages: in addition to having no advertisements, the paid version of this app allows a student to create melodies with more than twenty duration units.

Art and Music Apps for
Middle School Students (5–8)

How to Draw (Free Lessons)
Recommended Grade Levels: 5–12
Developer: Pacific Spirit Media
Website: none available for app; designer's webpage: www.pacificspiritmedia
    .com/
Cost: Free

This app includes eighteen instructive videos. No drawing is done on the iPad; the videos simply provide instruction so that the user can follow by drawing on paper. Figure 4.4 shows the beginning screen, which has the first video selected.

Tapping on any of the titles below a video brings up a window with a brief description of the selected video. Tap on a white arrow to begin viewing the instructive video. Each video can be made full screen and paused as needed. These videos can be played for full-class instruction. However, if individual iPads with earphones are available, students can pause as needed to have time to draw. The videos also provide a great resource for the flipped classroom. All the videos provided with this app are listed:

1. Pencil Drawing Techniques
2. Draw Bart Simpson

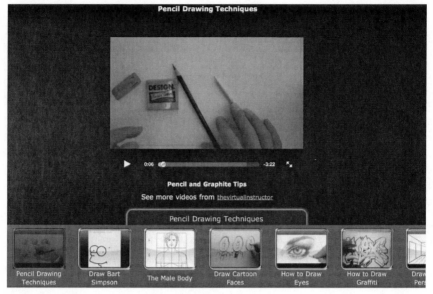

Figure 4.4. How to Draw—Opening Screen.
Image created by the author.

3. The Male Body
4. Draw Cartoon Faces
5. How to Draw Eyes
6. How to Draw Graffiti
7. Drawing with Perspective
8. Scenes with Perspective
9. How to Draw Faces
10. Drawing Flowers is Fun
11. Drawing a Face
12. Draw a Cartoon Tiger
13. Draw a Lamborghini
14. How to Draw Pokémon
15. Drawing Lips and Teeth
16. Draw 3D Letters
17. Drawing a Street View
18. Drawing Graffiti Letters

—⁓⁓⁓—

Beginner Guitar Songs
Recommended Grade Levels: 3–12
Developer: Guitar Jamz, Inc.

Website: www.guitarjamz.com/app/beginner_guitar_songs/#
Cost: Free

The guitar is arguably the most popular instrument to learn to play for middle school and high school students. For that reason alone, this app deserves to be on this short list of valuable apps for middle school students. This app is free and provides thirty videos, well sequenced to teach the beginning student the basics of playing the guitar. Each video shows Marty Schwartz of Guitar Jamz as he explains and demonstrates techniques on his guitars.

On the left menu are links to four areas for instruction. In the *Beginner Lesson Series*, there are eight lessons that vary in length from nearly six minutes to over thirteen minutes. The *Important Guitar Chords* section includes seven short videos of less than a minute each, explaining the following chords:

- E minor
- A major
- D major
- G major
- E major
- A minor
- C major

The *Strumming Patterns* section has six Rhythm Patterns videos of 1-1/2 to 2 minutes in length. Finally, the *Easy Guitar Songs* section includes nine songs of 2 to 7 minutes in length. For those who wish to follow Mr. Schwartz further, a button is provided in the lower left corner that allows the user to subscribe to a site with nine hundred free lessons. Mr. Schwarz also published an eBook and has a significant presence on YouTube.

—◦◦◦—

Drawing Box Free
Recommended Grade Levels: 5–12
Developer: Nguyen Tan Hon-Hu
Website: www.drawing-box.com/
Cost: Free

This app provides a wide range of possibilities for any budding artist. The opening screen shows a blank canvas with a menu at the bottom that provides eighteen different tools. Most of those options open a range of possibilities.

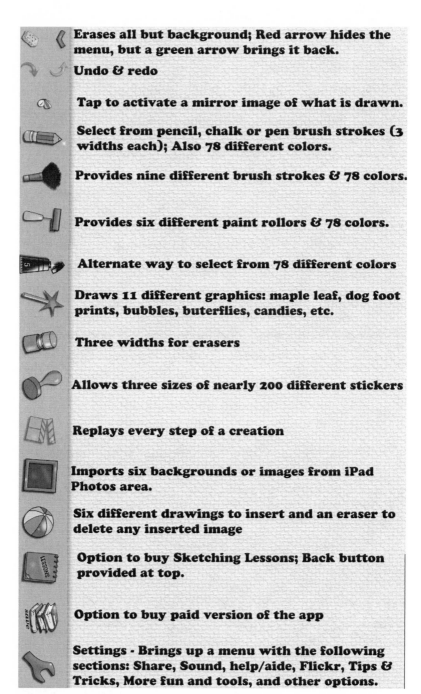

Erases all but background; Red arrow hides the menu, but a green arrow brings it back.

Undo & redo

Tap to activate a mirror image of what is drawn.

Select from pencil, chalk or pen brush strokes (3 widths each); Also 78 different colors.

Provides nine different brush strokes & 78 colors.

Provides six different paint rollors & 78 colors.

Alternate way to select from 78 different colors

Draws 11 different graphics: maple leaf, dog foot prints, bubbles, buterflies, candies, etc.

Three widths for erasers

Allows three sizes of nearly 200 different stickers

Replays every step of a creation

Imports six backgrounds or images from iPad Photos area.

Six different drawings to insert and an eraser to delete any inserted image

Option to buy Sketching Lessons; Back button provided at top.

Option to buy paid version of the app

Settings - Brings up a menu with the following sections: Share, Sound, help/aide, Flickr, Tips & Tricks, More fun and tools, and other options.

Figure 4.5. Drawing Box Menu Items.
Image created by the author.

Figure 4.5 shows the app's bottom menu rotated ninety degrees with a brief description added, for instruction about each item.

With that many options, the possibilities seem endless. A student can have great fun with this app creating an assortment of masterpieces.

—ᴡᴡ—

Learn the Orchestra
Recommended Grade Levels: 3–12
Developer: Sonic Network, Inc.
Website: none available for app; designer's webpage: www.sonivoxmi.com/
Cost: $1.99

The cartoon drawing of the orchestra on the opening screen might give the impression that this app is more appropriate for the elementary level. However, the hidden facts and quantity of information about all the instruments that make up the modern orchestra provide a valuable resource for upper-level music students. Several features of this app are certainly appropriate for use at the elementary level, but the quiz in particular is geared toward middle and high school students.

After briefly flashing the name of the app, the opening screen shows a cartoon drawing of a small orchestra with a conductor and thirty-four musicians. Despite the fact that the number is significantly smaller than today's orchestras, which can be about one hundred musicians, this orchestra still includes all major instruments. Below the cartoon are the icons to start, stop, and pause the playing of the piece listed at the bottom. The default is Beethoven's Symphony No. 5.

At any time, the conductor can also be tapped to either start or stop the recording. The user can also tap a section of the orchestra to mute that specific area. For example, in figure 4.6, the first violins have been muted, as shown by the faded color of the musicians. A student can listen to how the symphony would sound without specific sections of the orchestra.

Another instructive feature of this app allows a student to hear the sound of a specific instrument. This is done by tapping on the keyboard icon that is located in the upper left of the screen. A keyboard then appears in the lower section of the screen. Tapping in a specific section places a pink rug under all the similar instruments. In figure 4.6, the cellos have been selected. The user can tap on any of the notes of the keyboard and hear what the notes sound like when played on an instrument from the selected section.

Two icons appear in the upper right screen. The book icon brings up a booklet that explains the role of the conductor and describes each of the

Figure 4.6.   Showing First Violins Muted and Cellos Selected.
Image created by the author.

twenty-five instruments in the orchestra. Students can read the descriptions or they can tap on an icon in the upper left corner to listen to a recording of the words being read. Just to the right of the book icon is an icon of an award ribbon. Tapping there brings up a multiple-choice quiz. To be successful with the quiz, a student should first read and study the information in the book.

Overview video on YouTube: www.youtube.com/watch?v=gs0SrtHf-wM

—ᴗᴗ—

Go Go Xylo
Recommended Grade Levels: 3–12
Developer: Barrett Productions, LLC
Website: www.gogoxylo.com
Cost: Free

After a brief introductory page, the opening screen, as seen in figure 4.7, shows an artistic representation of a collection of instruments. By tapping in specific areas, a student can play the eighteen notes of the xylophone, ten notes from the blue clarinet, as well as notes from a tuba, a trumpet, a

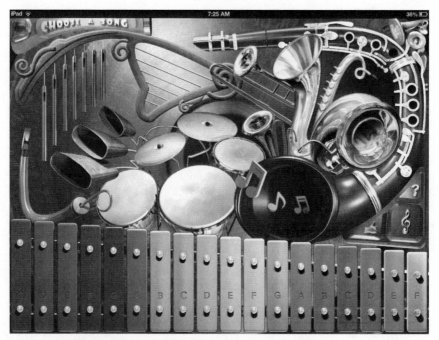

Figure 4.7.   Home Screen Allowing Free Play with Go Go Xylo.
Image created by the author.

trombone, a saxophone, a snare drum, two kettle drums, a six-string harp, two cymbals, and three percussion instruments.

The volume of the xylophone or the accompanying instruments can be adjusted by tapping on the two speakers in the upper right corner. Tapping on the *treble clef* on the lower right side brings up a window that allows for adjustments in keys. Tapping on the *question mark*, just above the treble clef, brings up some directions, along with a link to the YouTube tutorial: www .youtube.com/watch?v=HXqZe3IJxFU.

Tapping on *Choose A Song* at the top of the screen brings up a drop-down menu. Selecting *Free Play (Main Screen)* returns the user to the main screen. Below that are three songs. A link to *Download New Song* is at the top. Those songs are in two categories, classical or children, and vary in price from $0.99 to $2.99.

If a student selects the free song, "Baa, Baa, Black Sheep," new tools appear at the top and a music sheet appears above the xylophone. Ample instructions are provided there. Those instructions can be turned on and off by tapping on the *question mark* on the right side, above the xylophone. A student can learn a great deal about music with this app. Creativity is certainly encouraged.

Art and Music Apps for
High School Students (9–12)

Please realize that all of the previously mentioned middle school apps and several of the elementary level apps are also useful at the high school level.

———— ◈◈◈ ————

National Gallery of Art HD
Recommended Grade Levels: 9–12
Developer: Evolution Games LLP
Website: apps.ev-games.com/index.php/ngahd
Cost: Free

A search for *museum* in the App Store brings up apps for many of the most famous museums in the world. The National Gallery of Art certainly represents one of the best collections of artwork that this country has to offer. However, quite a few other museum apps are available. For some of the most famous museums, refer to the list at the end of this discussion about this app.

After briefly flashing its title, the home screen for the *National Gallery of Art* app brings up links to the museum's artwork sorted by century from the fourteenth through the nineteenth century. At the bottom of the screen are tabs to re-sort the artwork by *genre, style,* or *name,* or to return to the default setting of *century.* The *genre* arrangements provide eighteen different categories, including, for example, *Still Life, Pastoral, Portrait,* and *Landscape.* A few examples from the list of twenty styles are Baroque, Dutch, Gothic, Impressionism, Medieval, Renaissance, and Romanticism.

The listing by name is not alphabetical, but a search tool is provided at the top. This free app includes more than 920 paintings. The app shows the collection of images that appear when Claude Monet is selected. At the bottom of the screen, the option is provided to view the works as a list, rather than the thumbnails. With each list, the title is provided, as well as a link to view full screen.

Tapping on any one of the thumbnails also brings up a full-screen image with the name of the artist at top and the name of the work at the bottom. With full-screen views, there are six icons to tap at the bottom. Selecting the arrow on the left end of the menu brings up the menu that provides the six ways of saving or sharing the image, including downloading, saving to a PhotoAlbum, sending by e-mail, and publishing on Facebook or VKontakte. VKontakte is a popular European social network site.

The second link allows the user to e-mail a request to receive the high-definition image. The *HD* in the center of the menu enhances the quality of the image. The *i* to the right of the title provides a few more specifics about the painting. Below the *i* is an arrow that, when tapped, begins a slideshow, scrolling through all the images in the selected category. The user can also tap on the other arrows to move forward and backward through the images.

Amazingly, in addition to the collection of artwork, this app also has a selection of twenty classical pieces of music. Those are accessed by tapping on the menu icon, in the top left corner of the homepage; a dropdown menu provides the link to the music area.

The following is a list of seven apps for other internationally known museums. The museum's name and location is listed first, with the app's italicized name immediately following:

- The Louvre, Paris: *Louvre Art Gallery* by Evolution Games LLP, $0.99
- The British Museum, London: *British Museum* by Praveen Dandi, $2.99
- The Hermitage, St. Petersburg: *Hermitage Museum* by The State Hermitage Museum, Free
- The Grand Egyptian Museum, Cairo: *Egyptian Museum (Cairo)* by Egate IT Solutions Pvt. Ltd., $2.99
- Uffizi Gallery, Florence, Italy: *Uffizi* by Parallelo, $1.99
- Museum of Modern Art, New York City: *MoMA AB EX NY* by the Museum of Modern Art, Free
- The Museum of the Netherlands, Amsterdam: *Rijksmuseum* by Rijksmuseum Amsterdam, Free

—⁓—

Da Vinci HD
Recommended Grade Levels: 9–12
Developer: Boram Kim
Website: none available for app; designer's website: www.overdamped.com/
Cost: $0.99

After a brief introductory screen, the next page provides links to the following areas:

- Verrochio's Workshop, 1466–1476: Sixteen images of paintings and close-up images
- Professional Life, 1476–1513: Thirty images of paintings and close-up images

- Old Age, 1513–1519: Seven images of paintings and close-up images
- Battle of Anghiari: Eleven images of the painting and various related sketches
- Studies to Paintings: Twenty-nine images of sketches, with various levels of detail
- Head Studies: Fifteen images of amazingly detailed sketches
- Various Studies: Fourteen images of a variety of sketches
- Anatomica Studies: Thirteen images of drawings of human anatomy
- Study of Nature: Fifteen images of landscapes, plants, and animals sketches
- Maps and Architecture: Six images of structures and details
- Sculpture: Eleven images of photographs and sketches
- Bookmarks: Area where user can bookmark favorite images

Altogether, there are 167 images. Information is provided below each image, including the title, the date, the medium, the size, and the current location of the work. For example, the *Mona Lisa* has the following information:

"Mona Lisa (La Gioconda)," c. 1503–1505

Oil on panel, 77 X 53 cm

Musée du Louvre, Paris

That information usually covers a small section of the image, but the user can see a full view by tapping anywhere on the image. A second tap brings back the information and menu bars. On the lower menu bar are two arrows for scrolling through all the images within a specific section. Moving forward from the *Mona Lisa* are two close-up images of her face and also of her hands. This is perfect for a teacher to use for full-class discussions.

In the bottom right corner is an arrow that allows the user to save the image to photos, to save it to the *Bookmarks* section of the app, or to e-mail it. Just to the left of that arrow is a *W* button, which links the user to the Wikipedia page about that image. Internet must be available for that link to work. For some images, the *W* is not present, indicating that no Wikipedia page is available. To the left of the *W* is an arrow that begins a slideshow through all the images in the category. There are also two arrows for moving forward and backward within a category.

A *Music* button in the lower left corner plays classical music during the slideshow or through the viewing of any image. On the top menu bar, the category of an image is shown. To the right is an *All* button, which allows the user to see rows of all the images in that category. On the top left corner, the *Main* button returns the user to the main page.

As with the museum apps, many other apps are dedicated to a single artist. The following is a list of twelve such apps, representing some of the most famous artists. Often multiple apps were available for an artist; these twelve were selected based on a combination of price and quality. The artist's name is listed first, with the app's italicized name immediately following:

- Michelangelo di Lodovico Buonarroti Simoni: *Michelangelo HD* by Boram Kim, $0.99—Michelangelo's work is sorted into fifteen different categories.
- Claude Monet: *Claude Monet* by Hadron Solutions, Free—This app includes sixty-three famous paintings with biographical and other information.
- Edvard Munch: *The Artist—Edvard Munch* by Byungil Park, $0.99—More expensive apps are available, but this has good quality. This app includes fifty paintings and other sections about his motif and his biography.
- Pablo Picasso: *Pablo Picasso* by Wei Yao, Free—This app includes an interactive timeline and maps of museums where the paintings are located.
- Rembrant van Rijn: *Best of Rembrandt* by Nuno Palmeirim, $0.99—This app is fairly new and not yet rated, but it seems to be of high quality.
- Pierre-Auguste Renoir: *Renoir* by Wei Yao, $0.99—This app includes an interactive timeline and maps of museums where the paintings are located.
- John Singer Sargent: *Sargent HD* by Boram Kim, $0.99—This app focusing on the famous American portrait artist contains 412 paintings in ten categories.
- Georges-Pierre Seurat: *Seurat* by Wei Yao, $0.99—This app includes an interactive timeline and maps of museums where the paintings are located.
- Vincent Van Gogh: *Van Gogh* by Wei Yao, $0.99—This app includes an interactive timeline and maps of museums where the paintings are located.
- Diego Velázquez: *Velázquez HD* by Boram Kim, $0.99—Paintings are grouped into seven categories, ranging from 1616 to 1657.
- Jan Vermeer: *Vermeer HD* by Boram Kim, $0.99—Paintings are grouped into four categories, with a great deal of additional information.

- James Whistler: *Whistler* by Wei Yao, $0.99—The app includes an interactive timeline and maps of museums where the paintings are located.

———*&&&*———

Piano Infinity
Recommended Grade Levels: 9–12
Developer: Better Day Wireless, Inc.
Website: www.betterdaywireless.com
Cost: Free or $14.99

The first time that the app is opened, a message appears asking the user to buy additional features. After closing that message, the best place to start is by tapping on the *i* in the upper right corner, which leads to an *Extras* area that includes a *Tutorial*. That tutorial leads the user through twenty-seven screens that explain the various features of this app.

After watching the tutorial, the user can return to the home screen, where there are links to four different areas:

- Play
- Learn
- Create
- Jam

The *Play* area brings up a full eighty-eight key piano keyboard with the shaded region showing the currently playable keys, as shown in figure 4.8. The shaded area can be changed either by dragging the area left or right to the desired keys or by simply pressing the provided arrows. Other directions are provided for using the menu bar, changing the settings, and changing the type of keyboard.

In the *Learn* section, two columns are provided for the user to select between *Learn* and *Listen*. For the free app, those options are only provided for four songs. More than one thousand additional songs are available with an upgrade. With each of the four songs, the *Learn* area has four selections: theme (easy), both hands (expert), or left hard (bass clef) or right hand (treble clef). The *Listen* area has just three options: *theme (easy), both hands (expert),* and *complete song (theme + both hands).* The songs are played automatically in this area. Also in the top right corner, a heart with a plus sign allows the user to add the song to a favorites area.

In the *Learn* area, the next note to be played is colored in red and the music stops until the user plays the correct key. In addition to the colored keys,

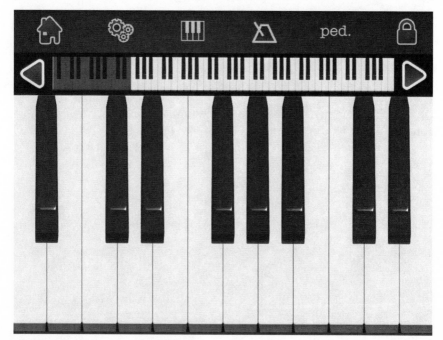

Figure 4.8.   Play Area of Piano Infinity.
Image created by the author.

orbs fall in line with the colored keys, providing timing for when the keys should to be pressed. Other settings are available. From the home screen, selecting the *Create* area allows users to record a song. Once a recording has been saved, the app provides instructions on how to edit the recording.

The final section on the home screen is *Jam*. There is no keyboard in that section, but rather only the falling orbs are on the screen. The user needs to tap on the orb at the right time. Further instructions for all areas of this app are accessible by tapping on that *i*, which is always at the top right of the home screen. This is the same information that was mentioned in the first paragraph, but it is handy to have it available at other times. The app has quite a few ways that adjustments can be made.

The only annoying feature with this app is the occasional appearance of messages that attempt to entice the user to upgrade. However, in all other respect, this is an excellent app for use in the music classroom.

YouTube: Titanic Theme on Piano Infinity www.youtube.com/
watch?v=ShYfQYewFgE

Music Tutor Free (Sight Reading Improve)
Recommended Grade Levels: 9–12
Developer: JSplash Apps
Website: www.facebook.com/musictutorapp
Cost: Free or $0.99 (also available on Android)

This app is essentially a series of timed practice quizzes that help the user learn to identify notes as they appear on the music staff. On the opening

Figure 4.9. Music Tutor Quiz in Progress.
Image created by the author.

screen, settings can be made to only show notes on the treble or bass notes or to show both types. Settings can also be made to set the duration of the quiz to one, five, or ten minutes. Users can also choose to have the sound of each note played or to have the sound muted.

As the quiz starts, a note is heard and that note also is shown on the staff, along with twelve possible answers below. As shown in figure 4.9, time, the score, and the percent accuracy are all shown at the top of the screen. After the quiz is completed, the user can review any mistakes that were made. The Review screen shows the original question, with the original answer and the correct answer.

The review screen also plays the sound of the note. As a student becomes familiar with the recognition of the notes on the staff, he or she can begin to practice the recognition of notes by sound only. By covering the staff and listening carefully to the sound, a student can select the correct note, as was done with the staff uncovered. Being able to recognize notes by sound is a skill valued by all musicians.

—᳁ᜥ᳁᳁—

Ratatap Drums Free
Recommended Grade Levels: 5–12
Developer: mode of expression, LLC
Website: ratatapdrums.com/
Cost: Free or $1.99

The main screen of this app, shown in figure 4.10, proves five drums, five cymbals, a percussion instrument, and one of two sticks that are ready to play. The user's finger serves as the second drumstick; the second drumstick appears briefly as each instrument is tapped. Also, with each tap, the user hears the sound as if the drumstick had actually hit the instrument. The user also has control of the volume: just as with real instruments, the harder an instrument is tapped, the louder the sound. Holding down on an instrument and moving your finger in a circle results in the sound of continuing short, quick hits, as with a drum roll.

A small tab is visible at the bottom center of the screen, with the word *ratatap*. To see the full menu, tap and drag upward. On that menu, the metronome settings are just to the right of the center tab. In all, 260 settings are available, ranging from forty to three hundred beats per minute. The next three icons allow the drummer to play, pause, and record sessions. The next icon activates looping, followed by an icon that brings up a way to adjust the

Figure 4.10.   Main Screen of Ratatap Drums.
Image created by the author.

loop length, from two to twelve measures, in addition to sixteen, twenty-four, and thirty-two measures.

The icon that looks like a cassette is for listening to recordings that have been saved. Another icon that looks like an iPod brings up a playlist, where songs can be added from several sources, including iTunes. The next to last icon provides a menu of fifteen different assortments of instruments that can be selected to replace the default setting. Taiko drums is just one of those assortments; a great variety is available. At the bottom of that pop-up menu is also where settings can be changed to adjust sounds even further.

The last icon on the ratatap menu brings up a window that provides the opportunity to upgrade. There are two advantages of upgrading to the $1.99 version. First is the absence of advertisements. Second, the upgrade allows users to edit their drum sets. That feature is shown during part of the You-Tube video: www.youtube.com/watch?v=7X2WzkV_gDI.

Additional Highly Rated Apps for High School Classrooms:
- *Classical Music l: Master's Collection Vol. 1* by Magic Anywhere, Free or $4.99—This app is highly rated, and includes 120 pieces, although the free version skips significant portions of some pieces. Links are provided to associated webpages on Wikipedia and YouTube.

- *ArtSite* by Learning Post Productions—Although this is labeled in the App Store as being free, that is just for a trial period. The actual cost is $9.99 per year. However, the app is highly rated and "allows students to create virtual galleries, find out some background on museum pieces, and comment on work of other students." (www.artsitenet.com/ Reviews.html)

Related Websites
- *Best iPad Apps in Art Education:* theteachingpalette.com/2013/03/26/ art-education-ipad-apps-which-ones-are-the-best/
- *12 Outstanding Music Teaching and Learning Apps for iPad:* www .educatorstechnology.com/2013/01/12-outstanding-music-teaching -and.html

Reflections on Chapter Four

How do the apps in this chapter relate to each of the words associated with the acronym *DEUCE*? Each of the words in that acronym comes into play throughout this chapter. For example, start by imaging the delight of watching a young student begin to discover the effects of mixing primary colors with the *Color Mixer* app. This is pure *discovery* learning.

Without exception, every app in this chapter is engaging. Young children are mesmerized by the *Art of Glow* app. With a set of set of earphones, an iPad, and the *Go Go Xylo* app, each student in a music class can be engaged throughout a class period learning to play the variety of instruments. Serious art students are equally engaged with learning all about the life and works of da Vinci.

As discussed in chapter 1, promoting understanding is the primary role of teachers. The teacher serves as the proverbial "guide on the side," while the apps in this chapter each serve as to tool that promotes the understanding. The *Music Tutor* allows students to understand the sounds and relationships between the notes on the treble and bass clef. An understanding perspective is taught as well in the *How to Draw* app.

Creativity remains an essential component in every one of these apps, as each app was designed with creativity and the creative ability of each user is allowed to flourish through the use of the apps. This is true for all the apps in this book, but even more so for the art and music apps of this chapter.

Finally, there remains no doubt that each of these apps can be used to enhance the learning experience of the user as he or she delves into the world of iPads. By no means can any of these apps fully replace the awesome experiences of being immersed in an art or music class. Only through the eyes of impassioned instructors, artists, and musicians can students begin to understand the joy associated within these realms of learning.

However, by introducing students to the apps included in this chapter, teachers and parents can personally fight back a bit against the tragic loss of instructional time for the arts happening in our schools today. Through the use of these apps, students can become absorbed in learning an appreciation of these two incredibly important areas of study.

CHAPTER FIVE

—ᧁᨆᧁ—

Teaching Health and Physical Education with the iPad

The Internet is teeming with articles about the obesity of U.S. school children. In 2012, the *Journal of the American Medical Association* reported that the number of obese adolescents had tripled from 1980 to 2010. In fact, more than one third of children ages six through nineteen were obese (Ogden et al., 2012). Those numbers are outright appalling! Both health education and some form of legitimate physical exercise should be a routine part of every school's curriculum.

A few years ago, the principal of a large public school in Nashville decided to try to provide more opportunities for his students to get some physical activity. He allocated ten minutes at the beginning of each day for walking outside the building. Unfortunately, entire classes of students were seen sluggishly sauntering down the school driveway; some students were barely walking. A slow, tedious, 10-minute walk does not achieve very much in the form of exercise. If an opportunity to walk fails to motivate students, perhaps these apps are just what are needed to achieve good health, either directly or indirectly.

An interesting perspective on the value of exercise comes form Sue Castle (n.d.), the executive producers of PBS Sports, who has been quoted as saying, "The evidence supporting sports participation for young people is overwhelming. . . . It has the power to combat everything from racism to low self-image, to the high-school drop-out rate." Valuing both the use of iPads and sports participation is not contradictory. The iPad apps that are included in this chapter support and encourage both exercise and sports participation in general.

The App Store offers a vast collection of fitness, health, and sports apps. To distribute them equally between elementary, middle, and high school is virtually impossible. So this chapter includes only two apps specific for elementary school students and then three more that have value for all grade levels. The remaining apps are probably most appropriate for middle school or high school students. Sixteen apps have full descriptions, with an additional fourteen listed as *Additional Valuable Apps*. In all, thirty apps are included in this chapter; each has significant value for coaches or for teachers of health and physical education (PE) classrooms.

—ɷɷɷ—

Health and Physical Education Apps for Elementary Students (K–4)

TGfU Games PE
Recommended Grade Levels: K–6
Developer: Nicholas Stratigopoulos
Website: educationisphysical.com/apps/tgfu-games-pe/
Cost: $1.99 (also available on Android)

The acronym *TGfU* stands for *Teaching Games for Understanding*. The TGfU organization represents the work of international educators and individuals who are "committed to the promotion and dissemination of scholarly inquiry around ways of knowing, learning and teaching through games-centered approaches" (TGfU, n.d.). Members of TGfU have published books about teaching games for understanding.

In addition, the organization holds annual international conferences. iTunes provides this description: "TGfU Games PE was developed to help physical and health education professionals incorporate fun in lessons aimed at keeping children active. TGfU Games PE combines technology, education, and fun to create an environment where children enjoy learning."

The app serves primarily as a resource for teachers and does not require iPad usage by the students. The opening page shows six main categories of games:

- Pursuit/Evade
- Invasion/Territorial
- Net/Wall
- Striking/Fielding
- Target/Misc
- By Sport

Hospital Tag

Recommended Grades:

Grades K-6

Equipment:

None needed.

Tactical Problems:

Tagging others, avoid getting tagged by others, and use of open space.

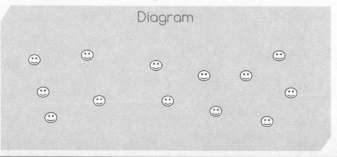

Rules of Play:

1. The basic rules are the same as tag.
2. However, you have "3 lives" so to speak.
3. The first time you get tagged, depending on where you get tagged (i.e. arm), you cannot use that body part anymore.
4. The second time you are tagged, that body part also becomes numb.
5. The third time you get tagged, you are sent to the hospital, which would be any area outside of the playing surface.
6. The game is over when there is only a few people left or if the instructor tells everyone in the hospital to get back in the playing area to restart the game.

Safety:

Keep your head up to avoid collisions and be aware of appropriate/soft tagging.

Variations/Progressions:

- Auto-defrost – Perform a certain number of repetitions of a physical activity to get back into the game after going to the hospital.
- After a certain number of players enter the hospital, they automatically re-enter the game.
- Players cover over their "wounds" the first and second time they are tagged with their hands, but still being able to move their body parts (cannot tag with hands covering wounds). On the third time they're tagged, they are sent to the hospital

Diagram

Figure 5.1. Description for Hospital Tag.
Image created by the author.

The first five categories have links to forty different games each. The "By Sport" listing simply provides a way to search for games appropriate for a specific sport.

Within each category, dozens of games are listed. Next to the title of each game, a target grade level is indicated. Most suggested grade levels seem appropriate, with the exception of grades 5 and 6 being listed for T-ball. The T-ball USA Association recommends it as appropriate for four- through eight-year-olds, which is PK–3rd grade (T-Ball USA Association, 2014).

Figure 5.1 shows one game from the Pursuit/Evade category. Every game on the app has a similar appearance. The title of the game, *Hospital Tag*, is at the top, along with the recommended grades. The equipment that may be needed is listed next, with *Tactical Problems* following. The designers want teachers to be aware of any problems that might occur with the specific game.

Rules of the Play, Safety issues to be aware of, and *Variations/Progression* are included with every game. Finally a *Diagram* of the positions that the players should take is always provided with this game. The equipment, such as cones, beanbag, and goals, are marked on the diagram, along with the position of players.

In total, descriptions of two hundred games are included with the app. As mentioned previously, the last category listed on the homepage is *By Sport*. The following is a list of the fifteen sports included in this app:

- Badminton
- Basketball
- Bowling
- Dodgeball
- Football
- Golf
- Hockey
- Lacrosse
- Multi-Sport
- Soccer
- Softball
- Tag
- Tennis
- Ultimate Frisbee
- Volleyball

Related Websites

- TGfU home website: tgfuinfo.weebly.com/
- TGfU history: tgfuinfo.weebly.com/history-of-sig.html
- YouTube video: www.youtube.com/watch?v=Awt6OIDVggg

—⚘⚘⚘—

Food Heroes
Recommended Grade Levels: K–4
Developer: BitCrew, LLC
Website: none available for app; designer's website www.thebitcrew.com
Cost: $1.99

Using this app, a student can begin to recognize healthy foods. The main menu provides three options: *match two, word puzzle,* and *coloring book.* The goal of the *match two* game is to match six sets of cards that show healthy foods. When a student taps on a card, the card flips and reveals the image of a healthy food item. After an initial tap, a timer begins on the side. If a match is made with a second selection, the two cards disappear. If no match

Figure 5.2.   Food and Heros Word Puzzle.
Image created by the author.

is made, the student can try again. There is a *Main Menu* link at the top to return to the opening screen, at any time.

The goal of the *word puzzle* is to find eight healthy foods listed on the right side of the screen. Figure 5.2 shows a puzzle in which seven words have been discovered and highlighted. As a student drags his or her finger across a newly discovered word, the word becomes highlighted. The image shows that only the word *meat* still needs to be located.

With each word, a sentence at the bottom of the screen with voiceover gives some specific information about the food. In figure 5.2, *cucumber* was the most recent word discovered. The sentence informs the student, "The inside of a cucumber growing on a vine can be 20 degrees cooler than the outside air on a warm day." When all the words have been located, a message pops up with the number of words found, the time taken to find the words, and the points earned for completing the game. The icon near the bottom right allows the user to toggle between *Find words* and the *stopwatch*.

The last section of this app is the *coloring book,* which initially brings up a whiteboard area for drawing freehand. However, tapping on the coloring book icon at the bottom right brings up six different pages, each with healthy foods. Colors are provided at the top, along with a pencil and eraser. Beware of the X on the top menu, as it deletes the entire page, not just the last step. Use the eraser to undo any unwanted markings.

Apps and Lessons for All Grade Levels (K–12)

Team Shake
Recommended Grade Levels: K–12
Developer: Rhine-O Enterprises
Website: www.rhine-o.com/iphone-apps/team-shake
Cost: $0.99 (also available on Android)

Hopefully, gym teachers are no longer asking students to pick their own teams. Allowing students to select teams is cruel to those who are not particularly athletic. This app eliminates student-chosen groups and also allows teachers to pick teams without any worry about being accused of being partial to or prejudiced against any particular student.

Figure 5.3 shows the main screen, a list of twenty-one students. Each student name is added by tapping on the plus sign in the upper right corner, which brings up a small window. The *Add New User!* window has room to type in the name of a student. If desired, the user can assess the *Contacts* area of the iPad.

Figure 5.3. Main Page for Team Shake.
Image created by the author.

At the bottom of the list of students is a scrollable area where the user may select from one team to sixty-four teams. After the students have been added and the number of desired teams is selected, then the user can either tap on the *Shake 'em Up* button at the bottom or simply shake the iPad itself. Either way, the teams are generated, based on the selections.

For example, if teams were generated with a selection for six teams from a group of twenty students, the *Team Shake* would generate the first two teams to have four students each and the remaining teams with only three students. If a teacher needs to have only a specific number on a team, with some possibly sitting out, then start by tapping on the arrows just to the left of the lists of teams. The selections then change to a range of one to sixty-four *people*, rather than one to sixty-four *teams*.

If, for some reason, a teacher notices that there is a potential problem with two of the students in a particular group, he or she can just shake the iPad again to redistribute the students throughout the same number of teams. On the *Teams* screen, tapping on the link in the lower right brings up a pop-up menu with three selections: *Share Teams as Text, Share Teams as Image,* or *Print Teams.*

Sharing a copied text can be done through e-mail or Facebook; the text can also be copied and pasted in another app, such as Evernote, Notes, or wherever text can be typed. Sharing as an image offers the same areas as the text, but also provides the options of printing or saving to the *Camera Roll* area. Several other features are worth exploring. Tapping on the *Manage Lists* button on the lower left of the main screen, brings up six options:

- Backup/Export
- Import List
- Create New List
- Load List
- Save New List
- Save List Changes

A final valuable feature is the app's ability to randomly choose one student from a list, which is accomplished by tapping on the button just to the left of the lower right *Share* button. Once tapped, the name of the single player appears. Tapping on the button a second time randomly selects another player.

⎯⚬⚬⚬⎯

Best Stopwatch
Recommended Grade Levels: K–12
Developer: Smartphoneware
Website: www.smartphoneware.com/stopwatch-for-ios-product.php
Cost: Free

At the App Store, a search for "stopwatch" brings up over two dozen apps. *Best Stopwatch* is one of the highest rated, and it also seems to have easy application to the gym or PE classroom. Most gym teachers already have stopwatches, but there always seems to be a need for more. This app provides a free way to access the features of a regular stopwatch, but, in addition, it has the capability of e-mailing the results, which certainly cannot be done with a regular stopwatch.

As the app opens, a large stopwatch covers the full screen, with numbers similar to those on an actual stopwatch. At the top of the screen is an area used to toggle between setting the stopwatch to show either the split times or the lap times. Below the center numbers are three buttons for *Start, Lap,* and *Reset*. After tapping on *Start*, the stopwatch begins to record the time. If the *Lap* mode was selected, the user can tap on the *Lap* button at the end of each lap. A set of numbers below the main area starts recording the time for a specific lap.

During the timing, the *Start* button is converted to the *Stop* button, indicating the end of a race or time period. The user then has a record of the total time and each successive lap time. A *Copy* button is also available that allows the user to copy and then paste the results into other applications available on the iPad, including e-mail. The times can be sent to the student, the parents, or the teacher to be saved for future reference. That is a fantastic feature that is not available with the standard stopwatch. Coaches might therefore prefer using the iPad at competitions, rather than the old traditional method of having to transfer times to a clipboard.

If the mode is set for split times, all the features function similarly. As the time progresses, the *Lap* button automatically changes to a *Split* button to tap at the end of each lap. The last feature simply allows for the ability to change the color of the stopwatch by tapping on the wrench in the upper left area. Five different colors are available. There is also an option there to upgrade to the $0.99 version that includes additional features.

Apps and Lessons for
Middle and High School Students (5–12)

AFIT
Recommended Grade Levels: 5–12
Developer: Thomas Watterson
Website: www.afitmodel.com/support.php
Cost: $1.99 or $4.99

The only negative for this app is the cost. The student version is $1.99 and teachers need to pay for the full version to track student progress. If funds are available, this app is a valuable tool to help students learn more about nutrition, as they track their daily consumption of healthy foods. The app also retains records of daily physical activity. The opening screen provides a way for a student to log in with a username and password provided by a class teacher or a group sponsor. The paid version also allows teachers to set up a classroom or group.

If no class or group has been set up, a student can start by tapping on the *Skip Login* button on the top right. The *Options* button at the top left allows a student to log-in at a later time. Figure 5.4 shows the main screen, with some tracking of nutrition and physical activity. The current day's date is displayed in the upper right by default, but, to view and make adjustments to previous dates, tapping on the button above the date can change the day.

As the user taps on a section of the plate, a pop-up menu provides a list of nutritional foods that meet the suggested daily consumption needs, as recommended by the Department of Health and Human Services and the U.S. Department of Agriculture (USDA). For example, at the top of the list of fruits is the statement, "Eat 2-1/2 cups each day." There are no adjustments made for age or weight, but that information goes a long way in bringing students closer to their specific needs. The Nutrition Log on the top right tracks the total daily servings of fruits, vegetables, grains, protein, and dairy foods. A five-day total is also calculated.

The mid-screen area shows eight glasses of water. The long-advised standard is that everyone should drink at least eight glasses of water daily. Each of those glasses can be tapped to indicate the consumption of that amount of water. However, remember that eight glasses is a minimum. The Mayo Clinic states, "You may need to modify your total fluid intake depending on how active you are, the climate you live in, [and] your health status" (Mayo Clinic, 2011).

The lower area of the app's screen tracks *Moderate and Vigorous Physical Activity (MVPA)*. Both activities and the associated time of each activity are recorded in this area. As above, the *Activity Log* tracks each activity that is entered. As an activity is entered, a recording of cheering is provided. A final valuable feature of this app is the link to the website, choosemyplate.com. A student can learn a great deal by reading various sections of this website.

Related Websites

- AFIT Pro App Tutorial on YouTube: www.youtube.com/watch?v=sNU QdzqaOFw

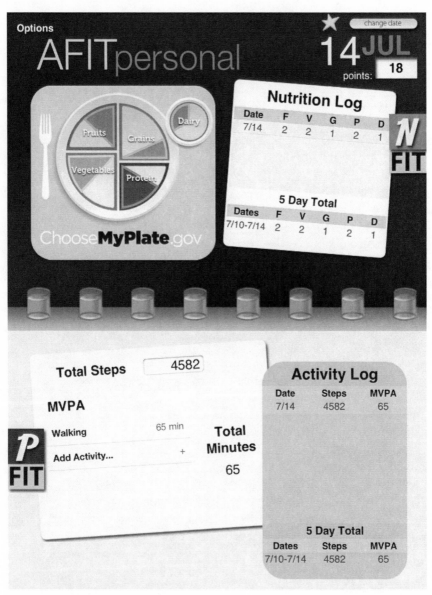

Figure 5.4. Main Screen for AFIT.
Image created by the author.

—⁓⁓—

Basketball Scoreboard Free
Recommended Grade Levels: 5–12
Developer: lab 9
Website: none available for app
Cost: Free

This app only applies to basketball. Scoreboards for other sports are listed at the end of this app description. When searching for this app in the App Store, be careful to choose the app by this designer, *lab 9*. Another app has a remarkably similar name, *Basketball Scoreboard. Free*, with the period after *Scoreboard* being the only difference. That app is by a different designer and is not quite as highly rated as this app by lab 9.

This app is a straightforward app that has obvious uses for any basketball coach. To set up the names of the competing teams, the user simply needs to tap on the tools icon near the top right of the screen. A window appears that allows for team names to be typed into the *Home* and *Guest* positions. There is also a possibility to set the times for both *Period Length* (8–20 minutes) and *Shot Clock* (24–35 seconds).

After saving the options on that screen, the user can start the time clock or the shot clock by simply tapping on the respective numbers. Tapping on the top part of the zero and every succeeding number increases the point total. If points need to be deducted for any reason, a scorekeeper can tap on the bottom part of the number.

There are four icons in the upper right area of the screen. The first switches the position of the Home and Guest teams. The second icon, which looks like a paintbrush, changes the background color. The tools icon, discussed previously, appears next. The information icon gives information about starting and stopping the time clock and increasing the team scores. Tapping on that button again returns the user to the main screen.

—⁓⁓—

Other Scoreboards Apps:
- *Scoreboard* (Free Version) by Sound House, LLC, Free—Has the advantage of being able to use a format for different sports, such as volleyball, basketball, football, hockey, baseball, rugby, badminton, and so on. However, it lacks some features available with apps that are specific to one sport.
- *Football Scoreboard* by Andy Edwards, $1.99

- *Real Cool Soccer Scoreboard* by Romel Gallamoza, $1.99
- *The Hockey Scoreboard* by Andy Edwards, $1.99
- *Tennis Scoreboard* by NIK, $0.99

⟶⟨⟩⟵

Nutrition Quiz: 600+ Facts, Myths & Diet Tips for Healthy Living
Recommended Grade Levels: 7–12
Developer: runtastic
Website: www.runtastic.com/en/nutrition/nutrition-quiz
Cost: Free or $1.99

This app opens with the image of a delightful salad composed of fresh lettuce and fruits. The user has four options: to *Sign in with Facebook,* to *Log in for members,* to *Join now,* or *Remind me later.* Before signing up for membership, the user can select the last option, which is at the bottom of the screen. After scrolling through three screens of enticements to join, the user can tap on the *Skip* button at the top right corner, which brings up the selection of choices shown in figure 5.5.

It is fun to take the quiz first, just to test one's knowledge. However, teachers usually prefer their students to tap on the *Categories* button, so students can learn about various facts, before initiating a quiz. Tapping on *Categories* brings up the following four options:

- Facts about functional foods
- Facts specific to either women or men
- Facts about sugar and spices
- Favorites, where the user's favorite facts can be added

Six additional categories can be added with an upgrade to the full version.

The *Quiz* opens an area with ten statements that correspond to information provided in one of the categories. As each statement appears, the user selects either *Fact* or *Myth.* After each question, the correct answer is provided. A user can select to save the answer to the *Favorites* category or the information can be shared through either Twitter or Facebook. At the end of the quiz the number of correct and wrong answers are shown. Points can be accumulated based on both accuracy and the speed at which answers are provided.

The *Settings* area provides the following six options:

- Enable/disable sounds
- Log in

Figure 5.5.   Nutrition Quiz.
Image created by the author.

- Rate us
- About
- Reset your personal statistics
- Notifications (if on: daily or weekly)

Considering the ability that this app has to keep a record of all quiz results, the app probably works best in one-to-one classrooms, but the *Reset* button allows that area to be cleared as needed. The total number of facts for the "Lite" version is about fifty, but substantially more facts are available both by logging in and by upgrading to the full version.

Emergency First Aid & Treatment
Recommended Grade Levels: 5–12
Developer: phoneflips
Website: none available for app; designer's website www.phoneflips.com
Cost: $0.99 (also available on Android)

The opening screen states, "This guide provides basic first aid and CPR information for the untrained, Trained Rescuer (TR) and for Healthcare Providers (HCP)." When the iPad is held horizontally, that message is at the top of the right column, above the *Emergency Action Plan (EAP)* area shown in figure 5.6. Held vertically, the iPad does not show the menu on the left. Five other important areas of advice are listed below the *EAP* on the right side.

In the left column is a list of fifty-four topics, mostly related to specific emergency events. The event listed at the top is *Emergencies: What to Do*, which is always associated with the information discussed previously. As a new topic is selected, the right column changes to the related information.

The last topic in the left column is *Support*, where the user can find additional information by going to the *Phoneflips* website or by e-mailing the company. The company webpage can also be accessed by tapping on the logo in the upper left corner. Unfortunately the items in the left column are *not* listed alphabetically. However, that can be easily changed by tapping on the switch button just to the right of the word *Contents* in the left column. The last icon above the left column brings up the following *Extras:*

- Emergency Numbers
- CPR Clock
- First Aid Refresher
- Video Channel

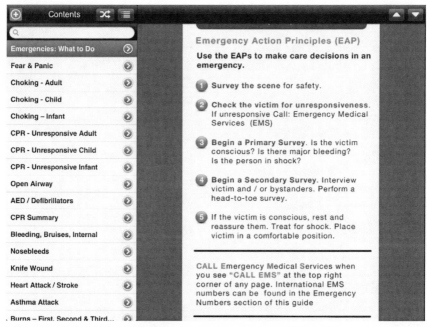

Figure 5.6. First Aid with Emergencies: What to Do Page Selected.
Image created by the author.

- Buy Medical Products
- Get CPR Trained
- Send Feedback
- Settings
- External Links

Overall there is a good quantity of information here that can be used for teaching young students the importance of emergency care.

——ⵡⵡ——

Soccer Trainer
Recommended Grade Levels: 7–12
Developer: iAmazing Apps
Website: www.iamazingapps.com/support.html
Cost: Free (also available on Android)

Through an ample collection of videos, this app can provide instruction for both coaches and students on ways to improve an athlete's ability to play the sport of soccer. After a brief introductory page, the opening screen offers five main areas. At the top, a *New Arrivals Area* provides two new drills.

However, the meat of the app is found in the next two sections: *Training Drills* and *Training Programs*. The *Training Drills* screen provides, at the top, a few *New Arrivals*, but the main *Training by Category* lists the following areas:

- Footwork
- Passing and Receiving
- Finishing
- Dribbling and Moves
- Juggling

Figure 5.7. Agility Ladder: Trainging Instructions in Soccor Trainer.
Image created by the author.

- Goalkeeping
- SAQ (speed, agility and quickness)
- Weight Training

Eleven videos are provided within the *Footwork* area. Figure 5.7 shows a snapshot of the *One Foot Zig Zag* video in the process of being played. The videos can also be played full screen. Textual information provided on the screen with each video includes the equipment needed, the setup requirements, and key points to keep in mind about the exercise.

The videos can be tagged as a favorite, if the user desires. The favorite videos are collected in the *Favorites* section that is linked from the homepage menu. As they are viewed, the videos are automatically checked as *Watched*. A coach can project these videos for full-class viewing. However, a student can also watch any of these videos on an individual iPad.

The *Training Programs* available from the home screen take a while to load because of the large collection of videos; ten different programs are currently available. Also from the home screen, this app provides links to nearly one hundred instruction videos on YouTube. Other areas available from the home screen include articles, a medical disclaimer, and information about the designers. Although this app is free, each area provides links to purchase collections of other videos that cost $4.99 for each set; some sets include as many as twenty-four videos.

—⁓—

MaxStatsFB13
Recommended Grade Levels: 7–12
Developer: MaxPreps Inc.
Website: support.maxpreps.com/
Cost: Free or $2.99 for MaxStatsFB13VE

The designer of this app describes it as "a real time statistics entry program for the iPad." The home screen provides links to four areas: *Start New Game*, *Continue Game in Progress*, *Show Games in Library*, and *Upgrade to the Varsity Edition*, which is called *MaxStatsFB13VE*. Both this app and the *Varsity Edition* have 13 in the name of the app to indicate the 2013 fall season. The designer upgrades the app annually.

New users should start by tapping on the tools icon in the lower right corner. Before anything is entered in this app, the user should set up *Member Login*, accessed from the top of that menu. Accounts are set up through the

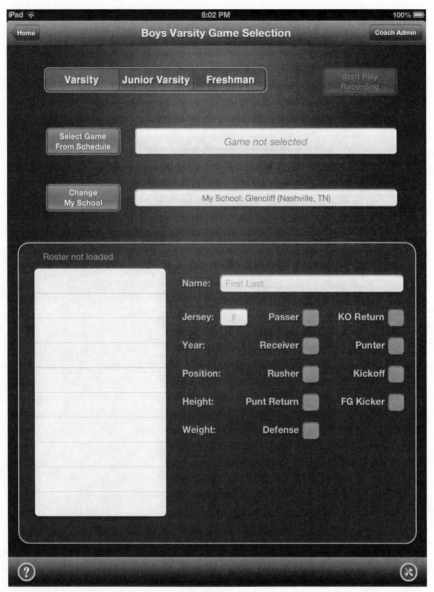

Figure 5.8.   MaxStats FB: Game Selection Page.
Image created by the author.

MaxPrep website. After establishing log in credentials, the next step is to tap on *Update Schools* and then select a state. After receiving the message that the schools for the selected state were updated, the user can then tap on the *Start New Game* tab.

The next screen is shown in figure 5.8. The first button is to select the team as being varsity, junior varsity, or freshman. Next tap on the *Change My School* button, which brings up a whole list of schools. If the state is not correct, then the state can be changed by tapping on the *States* button in the upper right. After selecting a school, the app returns to the page shown in figure 5.8.

Selecting a game is only possible during the seven days that precede a game. An important button, especially for beginning users, is the *Information* area, accessed by tapping on the question mark in the lower left corner. That brings up the app's *User Manual*, which has thorough directions for completing and using the app.

As each year passes, *MaxStats* develops a new app. So, in coming years, look for *MaxStatsFB14*, *MaxStatsFB15*, and so on. In addition to this app for football, *MaxStats* has created a great app for basketball, listed in the *Additional Valuable Apps* section at the end of this chapter.

—⁓—

GameChanger Scorekeeping and Live GameStream for Baseball, Softball and Basketball
Recommended Grade Levels: 7–12
Developer: GameChanger Media, Inc.
Website: www.gamechanger.io/
Cost: Free (also available on Android)

This app has been designed primarily for coaches and scorekeepers to keep a detailed record of every play of a game. The opening window of the app provides an instructional area that can be skipped as a user becomes familiar with the various features. After the introductory pages, the next screen provides four links:

- *Sign-in* button for those who have already registered
- *Score Game* button
- *Find Teams* button
- *Score a Practice Game* button

As with the previous app, a user must set up an account, either online or on the iPad. After that, a message appears that no teams are yet connected with the account. Tapping in the upper right corner opens up an area where the user can search for a team or create a team. *Help & Practice* appears here, as well as a link for signing out. An excellent area to start is the *Help & Practice*, which brings up a window with the following options:

- Video Tutorials
- Score a Practice Game
- E-mail Support
- Status

The *Video Tutorials* open up YouTube with access to a collection of ninety-two videos that all relate to this app, with titles *GC Demo* and the following subtitles:

- In-Game Scorekeeping, sixteen videos
- Getting Started and Team Setup, sixteen videos
- Post-Game Stats and Spray Charts, twelve videos
- Recent Uploads, sixteen videos
- Popular Uploads, sixteen videos
- Playlists, sixteen videos

Figure 5.9. GameChanger Practice Session.
Image created by the author.

The first video suggests that users step through a practice session. A snapshot of the first screen in that session is shown in figure 5.9 and is accessed by first tapping on *Help & Practice* and then selecting *Score a Practice Game*. As the majority of students are visual learners, videos have a very valid place in an instructor's tool bag. The extent of information provided with those videos makes it totally unnecessary to include any further instructions here.

⌇

Quit Pro: Your Smoking Cessation Coach
Recommended Grade Levels: 5–12
Developer: Bitsmedia Pte Ltd
Website: www.facebook.com/QuitPro
Cost: Free or $4.99

Smoking is a tragic habit that is most often started in the teenage years. An encouraging article reported "a 9 percent reduction in a single year in the number of teens currently smoking" (Gorman, 2012). That reduction was attributed to educating students at an early age, so that they do not even start smoking. Yet 5.6 percent of teens are still smoking and, as the article mentioned, "17 percent of high school seniors still graduate as smokers." The battle against smoking needs to continue with ardent fervor. Health classes need to stress the importance of this issue. This app is just another tool that can be used to combat the abhorrent addiction of smoking.

The app was actually designed for personal use to help smokers to quit smoking. Ideally, this app should be set up for a single user. However, the *Settings*, accessible from a link on the bottom menu, can be adjusted so that information posted by one student can later be adjusted by another student. The first user of the app needs to set up a profile based on the following information: (1) number of cigarettes smoked per day, (2) price of a pack, and (3) number of cigarettes per pack.

As new students open the app, the teacher can instruct them to tap on the *Settings* link to adjust the previous information. Nonsmokers can enter fictitious numbers for the number of cigarettes per day to see the results and associated information. As nonsmokers realize the cost and ill effects of smoking, they can become more informed, and hopefully confirm that they never want to start smoking. They also may encourage their smoking friends to quit.

A student can also make adjustments in a *Quit Plan*, which is immediately below the smoking profile. That area provides five options:

- Cut down date
- Cut down time
- Target number of cigs per day
- Cold Turkey
- Gradual Reduction

The remaining listings in the settings area include an option to set the *Stats* for either Sunday or Monday. Then five different *Alerts and Reminders* settings are also available.

After adjusting the settings, a student should tap on the *Progress* icon on the lower menu bar, which brings up an area shown with links to the following six areas:

- *Since you quit*: This icon shows the number of months or years since the student has quit. This is based on the settings. Tapping on the icon, shows the specific number of days.
- *Not smoked*: This icon shows the number of cigarettes that the student has *not* smoked since quitting.
- *Smoked*: If the *Quit Plan* in the settings area was set at *Cold Turkey*, then this offers congratulations for not smoking any cigarettes since quitting. Otherwise it shows the number of cigarettes smoked since starting a reduction plan.
- *Life gained*: This icon show the number of days or months that a student will likely have extended his or her life by quitting the specified number of days.
- *Money saved*: This area usually influences students the most. It shows the money that has been saved since quitting by not buying cigarettes.
- *Health Benefits*: These are shown only once the student has completely quit smoking. Those who have quit can see information such as, "After 5 years of quitting, your risk of stroke is dramatically reduced and your risk of mouth, throat, and esophagus cancer decreases."

With each of those six links, a share button is provided, if a student wants to e-mail that information to a smoking friend. The information also can be posted on Facebook. The final two areas linked from icons on the bottom menu are *Stats*, which brings up graphs, and *Motivation*, which provides fifteen statements of facts about the advantages of quitting. The app can be upgraded through the *Settings* area. Five advantages for the upgrade are listed, including the elimination of ad banners and also 170 motivational tips, rather than the fifteen available with the free version.

⚬⚬⚬

Truth about Drugs Online Education
Recommended Grade Levels: 7–12
Developer: Foundation for a Drug-Free World
Website: www.facebook.com/QuitProApp
Cost: Free or $4.99

As referenced on the iTunes page for this app, the best solution to this country's drug problems is "to reach young people with effective, fact-based drug education—before they start experimenting with drugs. Tweens, teens and young adults who know the facts about drugs are much less likely to start using them."

The home screen provides the directions to "Pull up to Enter the Classroom." After doing that, an image appears that shows the front of a classroom. Swiping to the left shows a bit more of the image.

Logging in can be done by tapping on the classroom chalkboard. The user can log in either a teacher or a student, or can select to explore the app; the log-in can be done at a later time. Below the classroom image is the lower menu bar with six icons:

- Home
- My Class
- Notice Board
- Notifications
- Resources
- More

The *Home* icon always returns the user to the initial classroom image. *My Class* brings up the page shown in figure 5.10. The left column of *My Class* offers a list of eighteen different lessons. Throughout the program, each lesson has videos, readings, class assignments, and homework assignments. The videos can be projected in the classroom or assignment for viewing at home. The last two lessons, not shown in the image at the right, are titled "Putting the Truth about Drugs to Use" and "End of Program Class and Graduation." That last lesson is the only exception to the format provided in the other lessons. That lesson provides more of a reflection on what has been learned.

The *My Class* section is the meat of this app; however, the next three areas are also very valuable. The *Notice Board* is an area where teachers can post messages for their students. The *Notification* area is for sending messages.

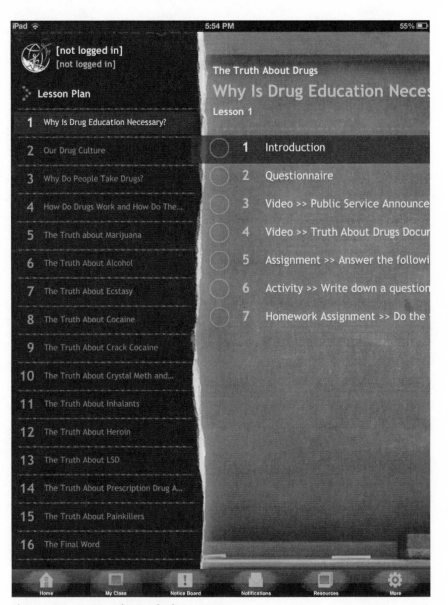

Figure 5.10. Lessons for Truth about Drugs.
Image created by the author.

The *Resources* area provides sixteen powerful films, different from those shown in the lessons. Each of the resource videos has individual teenagers relating how someone lied to them about the effects of drugs. Images show the consequences of having taken drugs.

This app and all the included videos have been developed by The Foundation for a Drug-Free World. The organization has its own website (www .drugfreeworld.org) and to reach more students and young adults, a Facebook group was created as a resource for those who register with the organization. Hopefully, schools will ensure that every teenager has an opportunity to complete this program sometime prior to being confronted with an offer to take an illicit drug.

Apps and Lessons for High School Students (9–12)

Fitness Trainer HD
Recommended Grade Levels: 9–12
Developer: Eltima
Website: fitness.eltima.com/
Cost: $1.99

iTunes claims that this is "the only tool you need other than yourself in the gym or at home." The app includes over four hundred exercises, each with images, as well as video, audio, and text instructions. This provides an incredible resource for any fitness instructor or weight trainer. Figure 5.11 shows a beginning screen with all the exercises listed on the left. By tapping on specific areas at the bottom of the screen, that list can be restricted to include only exercises to develop *muscles* or the full *body* or exercises that use *equipment*. There is also a link to a *my* workouts area, where custom exercises can be added.

On the right side of figure 5.11, the "45 Degree Calf Raise" is shown with a two-step description and also an image. The *Log this* button at the bottom right allows the user to record the reps and weight, as well as any additional notes. Although the default setting, shown on the top of the left column, is on *Exercises,* the user can tap on the *Workouts* button to change the list to twenty different workouts.

The home area is considered the *Training* area. Tapping of the *Log* button, on the top menu, brings up a list of all the exercises that were logged. There is also a calendar to correlate with those exercises. The *Tracker* area was designed for those who are trying to increase their body mass index (BMI). Twelve body measurements can be entered there. At the bottom of this area

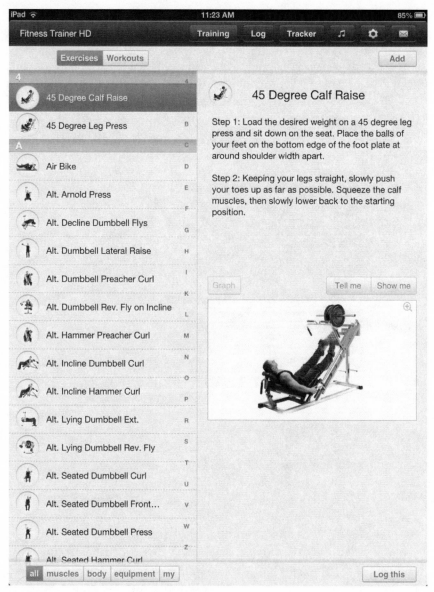

is a chart that can track BMI and show the results for one week, one month, three months, a year, or "all time." A calendar is provided to link back to the measurements for a specific day.

Next to the *Tracker* button is a musical note. When a user taps that button, music begins to play, which is being drawn from the iPad's iTunes play list. The next to last icon at the top allows for some *Preference* settings. The last icon, an envelope, sends an e-mail to the app designers with the subject of "in-app support request." The user can type any message that is needed.

Many of the areas of this app seem best for individual use. However, a coach can use the training area for planning exercises for a team or class. A teacher or coach can also project and show the videos accessible from the Training page. Two buttons appear above each image. The user or instructor can tap on the *Tell me* button to hear instructions. However, immediately also tapping on *Show me* allows a separate video to come up. A student can then watch the video while listening to the audio instructions.

——⋙——

Bracket Maker for iPad
Recommended Grade Levels: 9–12
Developer: Jacques Romano
Website: bracketmakerfortheipad.yolasite.com/
Cost: $0.99

This app generates brackets for single-, double-, or triple-elimination tournaments. In addition, Consolation and Compass tournaments can be bracketed, as well as Round Robins and Round Robins with Pools. A maximum of thirty-two players can be entered to fill up to four rounds. The best place to start with this app is by tapping on the *?* on the top menu bar. That brings up a window with twenty-two pages of thorough instructions, which really negates the need for much further explanation here.

The app opens with eight players already listed in the left column. Those can be deleted by tapping on the *Edit* button at the top left, which brings up negative signs by each name. Tapping on each negative sign and then on the delete button erases those names. As the user erases those names, warning signs may appear, but it does not prevent deleting all those names. Then tap in the box at the top that has the message *Enter Name to Add*. When all of the names are entered, tap on *Done* and then tap on *Copy to Brackets*. A warning appears that the previous names are being overwritten. The user can tap on the *Go Ahead* button.

Figure 5.12. Bracket Maker, Showing Brackets with Winners.
Image created by the author.

Figure 5.12 shows the names of thirty-two students distributed over a single-elimination bracket. Tapping on the icon between the question mark and the settings icon brings up a menu that includes going to a full screen. Once at the full screen, another pop-up menu can be access by holding a finger down firmly anywhere on the screen. That brings up a menu with the following seven options:

- Hide Game Numbers
- Enter Game Locations and Date
- Interact with Bracket
- Print Bracket
- E-mail Bracket
- Save Image to Photo Album
- Exit Full Screen

To fill up a bracket, student groups need to consist of exactly eight, sixteen, or thirty-two students. However, classes and groups of students rarely come in one of those exact numbers. The app resolves that issue by pairing certain students. For classroom activities, in an effort to involve everyone, an instructor can enter everyone's name and the app pairs students in such a way that some students are placed in the automatic position of winning a round. For example, if there were only twenty-seven students in a class, five players would be awarded an automatic position ahead of the remaining classmates.

Other features are built into this app and are all clearly explained in the information area, as mentioned earlier. Coaches especially should find this app to be invaluable.

—⁓—

Remind101
Recommended Grade Levels: 9–12
Developer: remind101
Website: www.remind101.com
Cost: Free (also available on Android)

This app allows both individual and group text messages or e-mails to be sent between teachers and students; all communications are done in a way in which neither the students or the teachers can see the actual phone numbers used. This is also an invaluable tool for the flipped classroom.

For coaches, it serves the critical need for communication. In the past, if an athlete was late to practice or to a game, the coach might call the central office and then page throughout the school to get the attention of a student as he sauntered through the halls. Now, very quickly, a message can be sent directly to the student, without the student ever having to share his number with the coach. More often, coaches can send reminders to all team members about upcoming events.

Setting up an account can be done on the web at remind101.com. In addition to the normal prefixes, one is also provided for "Coach." In addition to the name and e-mail, the coach or teacher needs to supply a password. On the website, e-mail and password is always needed to log in, but that information is saved on an iPad, so logging in is only required once.

After setting up an account, a coach can create a class or a team by opening the app and tapping on the *Add a new class* link on the left menu bar. If the menu bar is not showing, it can be brought out by tapping on the icon in the upper left of the screen. For every class added, an associated class code must also be created. A phone number is created that is specifically associated to the newly created account.

After creating a class, the coach can log into the class. To do so, open a new text message on any cell phone. Type in the phone number that *Re-*

mind101 provided. Then, in the message area, type in the code for the class, which always starts with @. Tapping on the *Subscribers* icon on the bottom menu of the app shows a list of the subscribers or members in the particular class. Messages can be sent to students by tapping on the *Message* icon at the bottom. Then click on the *Invite students and parents* link at the top.

A message appears on an e-mail. When a student receives the e-mail, a link is provide to a webpage that shows the student the phone number and code that should be used in the text message that allows the student to be a member of the *Remind101* team. Now the coach can quickly send messages to anyone who is a subscriber to the team.

Several videos are provided at the designer's website and also on You-Tube. Over a dozen videos that address specific features of *Remind101* are available at www.youtube.com/user/remind101.

Websites That Provide Lists of Apps for Teaching Physical Education
- *Using iPads in Physical Education: There Is an App for That!*—www.pelinks4u.org/articles/lleightNichols_1011.htm
- *Physical Education (PE) Apps for Teachers*—www.sparkpe.org/blog/physical-education-pe-apps-for-teachers/
- *Top 8 'Apps' for PE Teachers*—thepegeek.com/2011/03/28/top-8-iphone-apps-for-pe-teachers-part-2/
- *PE Apps for Teachers*—edtechideas.com/2011/09/16/pe-apps-for-teachers/

Additional Highly Rated Apps for Health or Physical Education Classrooms
The following are some excellent apps that did not make the list because of cost or similarity to another app:

- *Foodle—Nutrition Facts* by Pomegranate Apps, $6.99—This app was updated in May of 2013 to include, according to iTunes, "the entire USDA National Nutrient Database of over 8,000 foods!" Unfortunately the cost is somewhat prohibitive for full class usage, but, for a single user, it provides excellent information. If funds are available it can serve as an excellent resource for cooperative groups.
- *Coach's Eye* by TechSmith Corporation, $4.99—This is an awesome app that allows coaches to record videos of their athletes and then zoom in to show details. Coaches can show their athletes where improvements in techniques need to be made. This method of "mobile video analysis" is valuable for coaches of all sports. The price prevented

a full description in this book. However, the price is not excessive, considering that each coach would only need to purchase one app.

- *Tackle Football Playmaker* by TRUE, Free—iTunes describes this app as "an interactive playbook & quarterback wristband system designed by two championship-winning football coaches." The app is highly rated.
- *FirstDown PlayBook Dropback* by 1st Down Technologies, Free to download; associated costs—It's a great idea to have a mobile playbook. However, costs vary from $1.99/month or $4.99–$19.99 per PlayPack. The app is not as highly rated as the previous app, presumably because of the cost.
- *The 7 Minute Workout* by UOVO, Free—This app is more for individual use, but is highly rated and an excellent app to share with students. Related website: well.blogs.nytimes.com/2013/05/09/the-scientific-7-minute-workout/?_r=0
- *Beep Test Slim* by Simon Taylor, $2.99—This app is excellent for training. Beep Test Trainer ($3.99) and Beep Test Team Trainer ($4.99) apps are also available.
- *Basketball Coach* by Zappasoft Pty Ltd., $2.99—Apps also available are *Soccer Coach, Tennis Coach,* and *Swim Coach.*
- *PE Plus* by FinchMob Productions, $2.99
- *MaxStatsBB13, or 14 or 15* by MaxPreps, Inc., Free—This app is for basketball and was created by the same designer as the MaxStatsFB app for football.

Reflections on Chapter 5

A recent online article summarized Peyton Manning's thoughts about using the iPad as a tool for his profession:

> The ability to study both the playbook and game film on one device eliminates excuses for a lack of preparedness. Considering how the iPad can be so versatile and portable, and how it can be programmed to block certain web sites and scrubbed remotely if lost or stolen, it would not be a surprise if all 32 teams had some form of tablet technology by 2013. Rules now allow the devices to be used in locker rooms right up until kickoff, so there's no sense in wasting resources on paper playbooks. (McIntyre, 2012)

The value of the iPad and other tablet devices in the sports arena continues to be recognized. This chapter includes over thirty apps that each has significant value for coaches, as well as teachers in all health and PE classrooms.

CHAPTER SIX

—*ↄↄↄ*—

Teaching English Language Learners with the iPad

The dramatic rate of growth of English Language Learner (ELL) populations in the United States remains the norm and shows no indication of slowing. A recent article in the *Washington Post* stated, "Approximately 4.5 million English Learners are enrolled in public schools across the country, roughly 10 percent of all students enrolled in K–12 schools in the United States. The number of English Learners has increased by over 50 percent in the last decade" (Strauss, 2012). Those numbers explain the dreadful shortage of ELL certified teachers. Most school systems have had to resort to assigning teachers to those classes who do not have ELL certification.

Whether certified or not, teachers can use the iPad as a tremendous tool to address specific needs in this area. ELL students, even more than regular students, need visual reinforcements for the topics being addressed. Virtually all apps provide visual reinforcements with photographs, sketches, diagrams, and videos. The very nature of apps requires the use of more than just pages of text. Even the textbook apps are replete with images, voiceovers, and other features. In addition, teachers can project YouTube and other videos from the iPad. Google provides a YouTube app and Safari works very effectively with those videos.

In addition to being able to enhance learning visually, the audio features of the iPad can significantly enhance the learning experiences for ELL learners. Many apps have features that allow students to hear correct pronunciations. The value of those recording features cannot be overstated. Each of the five new apps listed in this chapter, as well as apps in the long list of *Previously*

Listed Apps, have recordings for correct pronunciation of letters, word parts, or full words. Being able to hear correct pronunciation is of paramount importance for ELL learners.

Another reason that the iPad is such a valuable tool for ELL teachers is the ease with which the device can facilitate cooperative learning experiences. One article titled *Using the iPad in ESL Learning* mentioned that "the iPad naturally lends itself to cooperative learning. The students can break into pairs or groups. . . . This greatly enhances their ability to learn" (Stevens, 2011). Even with just a small number of iPads, teachers can divide the class into groups, each with its own assigned device.

By its very nature, the ELL classroom has a wide range of needs. Students who have just arrived in the country, with no previous training in English, are usually placed in the same class as those with more advanced experience. Teachers often struggle with this disparity. The range becomes even wider when a new arrival, with no English skills, is placed in the classroom with students who have been speaking English from birth. This is the norm for classes such as music, art and physical education.

The flipped classroom can provide an excellent solution by meeting individual needs. This strategy allows ELL students to work at their own pace at home, without distractions from others in the class who may be able to work at a faster pace. Apps such as *Educreations* and *Edmodo* allow students to absorb a basic understanding of new concepts while at home. Individual assistance can also be provided at home through the use of *Remind101*.

After being introduced to topics at home, the classroom time for flipped classrooms is spent working on the material that was originally assigned as homework. Students can practice speaking with peers and receive individual help from the teacher. Also, teachers can immediately address any questions that perplexed students the night before. Flipped classrooms include strategies for students to contact the teacher from home, through e-mail or even the phone. That one-on-one guidance has been shown to greatly enhance learning.

The following is a list of five apps particularly designed to enhance the teaching and learning experiences in ELL classrooms. However, a multitude of other apps also have value for ELL learners; many of those have already been addressed in other chapters of this two-book set. After the descriptions of five new apps is a more extensive list of previously discussed apps, each with a brief explanation of how the app could be used specifically for an ELL class. Finally, there is a list of a few *Additional Highly Rated Apps for English Language Learners*.

Regular classroom teachers of all subject areas should particularly note the *Google Translate* app that has tremendous value for ELL students who may be placed in a class with native English speakers. Both regular classroom teachers, as well as those certified to work with ELL students, can find substantial benefits by using apps described and listed in this chapter. Altogether over forty different apps are included, each having significant value for the ELL student.

New Apps with Particular Value to the ELL Curriculum

Rocket Spellers
Recommended Level: Beginner and Low Intermediate
Developer: Little Big Thinkers
Website: littlebigthinkers.com/
Cost: Free or $2.99

Certainly for young learners, this provides an engaging way to promote spelling skills. Five levels of difficulty are included, with the default being initially set at the lowest level. Immediately after the arrow is pressed to start this app, a screen appears similar to figure 6.1, with a green alien in a rocket ship. An image of the word is shown on the right, as the alien pronounces the word. For the lowest setting, that word can be as small as three letters to as many as six letters. The letters in the word are scrambled at the bottom of the screen, as shown in figure 6.1. As the student drags each letter to the correct position, the alien says the name of the letter again.

If a letter is moved to an incorrect position, it immediately bounces back. After all the letters are placed in the correct position, the alien pronounces each letter again, then repeats the word before turning and flying off to the next screen. After three words are spelled correctly, the student selects one of three sections of a rocket. After twelve words are spelled, the three selected rocket parts self-assemble and the little green alien climbs aboard. As soon as a student is ready, he or she can launch the rocket by pressing on the red launch button.

The icon in the lower right corner of the home screen takes the user to the settings area where users can select to have either uppercase or lowercase lettering. Also the level of difficulty can be adjusted. With the increasing difficulty of each level, some features change, as discussed here:

- Level 1 consists of three- to six-letter words. Letters are placed in any order. Audible and visual hints are available. Four different rocket parts are available to select from after each group of three words is spelling correctly.

Figure 6.1. Rocket Spellers: Simple Level 1 Word.
Image created by the author.

- Level 2 consists of three- to ten-letter words. Correct order is required. Audible and visual hints are available. After each group of three words is spelled correctly, the user can select from five different rocket parts.
- Level 3 consists of three- to four-letter words. Correct order is required. Audible hints are available. Adaptive assistance is also available. Six different rocket parts are available for selection after each group of three words is spelled correctly.
- Level 4 consists of five- to six-letter words. Correct order is required. Only adaptive assistance is available. Seven different rocket parts are available for selection after each group of three words is spelled correctly.
- Level 5 consists of seven- to ten-letter words. Correct order is required. Only adaptive assistance is available. Eight different rocket parts are available for selection after each group of three words is spelled correctly.

Only the first two levels have the shaded letters provided as hints. Only Level 1 allows students to select the letters in any order, as long as the letters are placed in the correct position. When the adaptive assistance is present, hints are provided only as needed. Spelling can be very intimidating for young learners, but this app adds some levity to the task. Building and launching rockets serve as an engaging reward system. As the rocket launches, the student hears background sounds of cheers and applause. The full version of this app provides over 450 words.

—⟨ω⟩—

Kidioms
Recommended Levels: High Beginning and above
Developer: Ventura Educational Systems
Website: www.venturaes.com/ipadapps/kidioms.asp
Cost: $1.99

Understanding American idioms presents a significant challenge for ELL students of all ages, but this app goes a long way to ease the process of learning sixty-four well-known idioms. The opening screen provides links to *Settings*, *About*, and *Start*. The designer had some fun by designing all the links throughout the app to appear as large wooden clothing buttons. Certainly, ELL students might not be aware that the word "button" refers both to an article on clothing for clasping, as well as a device for triggering an electronic response.

The *Settings* area is for toggling the sound effects and the speech effects on or off. The *About* area serves as an introduction page for the app, with an explanation of the word *idiom* and an example of "raining cats and dogs." Pressing on the *Start* button brings up the screen shown in figure 6.2.

Throughout this app, each idiom has its own page. Below the idiom, a *Meaning* section succinctly explains the meaning and an *Example* section shows how it is used within a short paragraph. Altogether sixty-four idioms are included in what appears to be a sixty-four-page spiral notebook. Users can simply tap on a page to access the next idiom. There is also a scroll bar at the bottom that allows users to scroll through the pages, but it is difficult to use when moving just a few pages.

The buttons shown on each page link to separate game areas that allow for practice with the various idioms. Those games should not be started until the user has read through the notebook. The *Word Drop* game offers a screen with five words at the top. An idiom is below with a missing word. The student is expected to drag or "drop" the correct word into the missing space. An incorrect selection just jumps back to its original location as a star is taken away. A correct selection adds a star. Tapping on the screen then

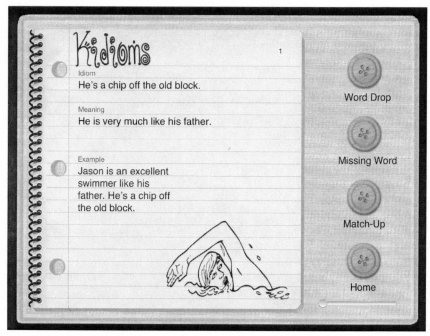

Figure 6.2. First Idiom.
Image created by the author.

shows a new idiom with a missing word and again five words at the top from which to choose.

The *Missing Word* game again shows one of the idioms with one word missing. However, for this game, empty boxes are below that correspond to the number of letters in the missing word. Then the twenty-six letters of the alphabet surround the entire area. A student can tap on letters in any order. With each selection, a recording provides the name of the letter.

If a needed letter is selected, it moves from the border area into one of the provided boxes. With incorrect selections, the letter simply disappears. After each word is completed, a number appears in the box in the lower area of the screen that corresponds to the number of points earned. Correct selections earn three points, while incorrect selections lose a point.

The *Match Up* game has the idiom at the top with a portion of the expression missing. Students are provided with five possible phrases that could possibly complete the idiom. Students simply tap on a selected answer. A correct selection brings up a star and a recording of "That's correct" or "Super" or several other similar affirmations. For this game, the box in the lower area shows the item number out of ten and the percent correct. Tapping on the screen brings up the next question. An incorrect answer takes away a star and proceeds to the next question; the percent grade reflects the missed answer. The designer also provides a *Kidioms II* and *Kidioms III*, both at $1.99. Purchasing all three apps may seem expensive, but quality apps like these are not "a dime a dozen." After practicing with these apps, ELL students will be able to understand and use idioms "at the drop of a hat."

—◈◈◈—

Google Translate
Recommended Levels: All levels
Developer: Google, Inc.
Website: support.google.com/translate/answer/1075927?p=iosapp_about&hl
   =en&rd=1
Cost: Free (also available on Android)

Without a doubt, this app is a must-have not only for every ELL classroom, but also for every classroom that has one or more ELL students. The app is straightforward, and functions similar to the translate.google.com website, only with additional valuable features. When a teacher has a student who does not have a shred of knowledge of the English language, the teacher can place the iPad in front of the student and type in the message such as the one shown in figure 6.3.

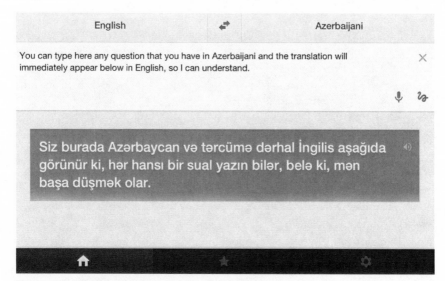

Figure 6.3.   English Text Translated to Azerbaijani.
Image created by the author.

If, for example, a student is from Azerbaijan, then he or she can understand the text. The teacher can switch the English to the right side of the top bar and then the student would be able to type a question back to the teacher. This feature is available in over seventy languages and that number is likely to increase with each update.

ELL teachers know that many foreign students come to this country without an ability to write even in their spoken language. Many countries do not provide schooling for everyone, as is done in this country. The Google Translate app addresses that issue by allowing a student to tap on the microphone on the right side and then speak the question. The text almost immediately appears along with the translation. Unfortunately, the spoken language input is not available for all languages. When it is not available, the microphone is faded. However, Google Translate continues to add other languages.

A handwritten feature is also available by tapping on the handwriting icon located just to the right of the microphone. Again, not all languages are supported and the icon is faded when this feature is not available. A *Settings* area is accessible from the lower menu bar, as well as a *Star* area. When a teacher types a question that may be needed again, he or she can then tap on the star, which stores it for later use in the *Star* area. A few other features are included. Any teacher who works with ELL students should find this app invaluable.

Apps for ELL Students Aspiring to Attend College

For ELL students who wish to enter a university, two main English language tests are accepted by most universities: Test of English as a Foreign Language (TOEFL) and International English Language Testing Service (IELTS). The TOEFL tests are administered by the Education Testing System (ETS) and are therefore more prevalent in the United States. Three separate groups administer the IELTS jointly: the British Council, the University of Cambridge ESOL Examinations, and IDP Education Australia.

However, selecting the best test may not be as simple as basing it on the student's country of residence. Despite the fact that the IELTS test has some variations in spelling that can cause a problem for some U.S. students, it has been growing in popularity and is reportedly "the world's most popular English proficiency test for higher education" (PRNewswire, 2013). For the individual learner, the i-studentglobal website (www.i-studentglobal.com/ learning-english/ielts-vs-toefl-which-is-better) compares the two tests' differences in structure.

Both a TOEFL and an IELTS app are discussed in this section. Teachers should always be supportive of students who want to attend college. Both these apps provide considerable practice for being successful on the respective exams. However, the words and practice sessions that are provided with these apps can also help all students to be successful on classroom tests, as well as on state ELL tests. All ELL students in the upper levels of learning could benefit through the use of these apps. Teachers could use the apps for whole-class discussion or iPads could be set aside for individual use.

——⁓——

TOEFL-TOEIC Vocabulary
Recommended Levels: High Intermediate–Advanced Proficient
Developer: Du Nguyen
Website: none available for app; designer's website: www.fasttest.me/
Cost: Free (also available on Android)

The opening screen of this app offers ten groups of words, with two hundred words in each group. Two thousand words are provided with this app and a button is provided to sort the words randomly if desired. Tapping on any particular group brings up a screen in which each of the words is shown with two or more synonyms. For example, below the word *enthusiastic* are the words *eager* and *ardent*.

A blue arrow is placed below each group listing of twenty words. Tapping on the arrow brings up a quiz, starting with a word shown at the top, such as *rugged*. Students can tap on a microphone icon below to hear the word *rugged* as it should be pronounced. Four possible groupings of words are shown, with one being the correct synonym group for *rugged*. If the correct answer is chosen, it is highlighted in lime green and a recording plays the word. If an incorrect answer is selected, the correct answer is again highlighted in lime green, but the selected answer is highlighted in rose.

The top section is not always the word. Often the definition such as *eager, ardent* is displayed and the word must be selected. Occasionally, the quiz provides a word with letters missing, as shown in figure 6.4. Sometimes all but one of the letters are missing and the definition is provided. Students are expected to tap in the correct letters in sequence, based purely on the synonyms that appear below. All questions color incorrect answers in rose and correct answers in lime green. Twenty questions are on each quiz and they get more difficult as the student proceeds through the quiz, with a goal to show a thorough understand of each group.

Figure 6.4. Quiz Question with Missing Letters.
Image created by the author.

The home screen also indicates the number of *Learned Words* out of the two thousand total. There is also a menu bar at the bottom of the home screen with three selections. The *Home* area always provides the group listings, as mentioned previously. The *Settings* area allows the user to turn off the sound and the pronunciation recordings. A button for clearing studying history is also available there.

Finally, the *About* button brings up a page with three other buttons labeled *Check out other apps*, *Visit www.fasttest.me*, and *Give us your review*.

The middle link brings up a website with links to practice tests for TOEFL, IELTS, and the Law School Admission Test. Again, this app definitely has value for all ELL students, whether or not they plan to take the TOEFL.

————*∅∅*————

Additional Highly Rated TOEFL Apps

- *TOEFL iBT, Preparation* by XuVi, Free (ourstudyhub.com/pre_toefl/)— This app helps to prepare students for the Internet-based TOEFL. The designer focuses on vocabulary from across all subject areas and has also designed a *Preparation 2* app.
- *TOEFL Speaking* by XuVi, Free—This app has the same designer as the previous app, but this one focuses solely on the speaking section of TOEFL, where students need to make recordings to be evaluated by an ETS examiner. For many students, this is the most intimidating section of the test. This app offers plenty of practice and thus can help to build confidence.
- *TOEFL Essay Preparation HD* by Shijun Zhou, $1.99—The focus here is for students to improve their writing skills to have success on the essay portion of the test.

————*∅∅*————

IELTS Skills—Free
Recommended Levels: High Intermediate–Advanced Proficient
Developer: Macmillan Education
Website: www.macmillaneducationapps.com/
Cost: Free (also available on Android)

As of the fall of 2013, two dozen IELTS-related apps are listed in the App Store. One is discussed here and several others are listed later in this chapter. This app was chosen above the others because of its high rating and its ability to provide "sample content" from four other for-pay apps also developed by MacMillan. In essence, this app is a teaser for other MacMillan apps. However, teachers and students can use this app, become familiar with the format, and then make a determination whether to buy the others.

Also, with this app, students can discover their own strengths and weaknesses. If a student excels, for example, in the *Reading* area, but shows weakness in one or two other areas, then that information would allow the student to wisely choose the best additional app from the following list. This series of apps is produced by MacMillan Education and is based on two best selling books by Sam McCarter (*Ready for IELTS* and *Tips for IELTS*).

The Home screen for *IELTS Skills* provides links to five areas:

- Reading
- Listening
- Speaking
- Writing
- More about IELTS Skills Apps

The *More about* section explains the MacMillan series. Each of the other four areas proceed to a window that has a menu with links to six specific areas. For example, the Reading areas are:

- Skimming for Content Words
- Skimming for Connecting Words
- Completing Summaries
- Using Grammar
- The Language Used in Claims
- More about IETS Skills Apps

In the *Skimming for Content Words* section, the student is given an explanation how to read for understanding by focusing on the content and ignoring small functional words such as *at, in, the,* and *for*. When the *play* button is tapped, a paragraph appears and the words in the paragraph begin to disappear, forcing the reader to read quickly. Settings are provided for the words to fall away at a slow, medium, or fast pace. The student should read for understanding, as below the paragraph five questions must be answered.

In a paragraph titled "The Disappearance of Small Shops," each of the five multiple-choice questions shown below provides two or three possible answers, as listed here in each "Selection of Answers" section. The student needs to have a good understanding of the reading in order to select the correct answer.

1. Look at the title of the reading passage and decide whether the word *disappearance* is positive or negative. *Selection of Answers:* positive; negative
2. Look again at the title of the reading passage and decide what type of structure the reading passage is likely to be. *Selection of Answers:* A history of small shops; Classification of types of shops; A problem and solution

3. Skim Section 1 of the reading passage and decide what it presents. *Selection of Answers:* A cause; A problem; A solution
4. Which words in the first sentence of Section 1 are important to establish the answer in question 3? *Selection of Answers:* many small independent shops; is changing dramatically; national or multinational chains
5. Decide whether the disappearance of shops has a *Selection of Answers:* National and social dimension; local and social dimension; international and social dimension

Each of those five questions requires a good understanding of the English language. The words that were in the paragraph are not available to check answers, so it remains important that the students understand what they have read. After selecting the answers, three buttons are provided at the bottom. The *Check* button displays a green check mark by the correct answers or a red "X" by the incorrect ones. Corrections can be made before proceeding to the next screen.

In the *Skimming for Connecting Words* section, a paragraph is provided with eight missing words or expressions. Those eight are shown in an area at the top of the paragraph. As a student taps on a word, it darkens. The student should then tap on the area where the word should be placed and the selected word moves there. The *Completing Summaries* area is next and is similar to the last area, but students need to type in specific words from the paragraph.

Altogether this free app provides twenty different exercises, each with different activities. This is an excellent app to assess a student's strengths and weaknesses.

—*ww*—

Additional Highly Rated IELTS apps by MacMillan Education
- IELTS Skills: Reading—$1.99
- IELTS Skills: Listening— $1.99
- IELTS Skills: Speaking—$1.99
- IELTS Skills: Writing—$1.99
- IELTS Skills: Complete—$5.99 (a combination of all the apps)

Related Websites:
- IELTS Skills: Brand new apps from Macmillan Education (www.you tube.com/watch?v=U5ITtpeD_iY)

- IELTS vs TOEFL: Comparison of the test for individual learners (www .i-studentglobal.com/learning-english/ielts-vs-toefl-which-is-better)

—*ꙮ*—

Additional Highly Rated IELTS Apps:
- *IELTS Essay Builder* by Shijun Zhou, $1.99—Even with advanced learners, writing an essay requires a great deal of training and encouragement. This app provides an excellent resource for learning to write a high-quality essay.
- *IELTS Preparation* by XuVi, Free—Four thousand vocabulary words are included.
- *IELTS Study English* by Bui Duong, Free—Video lectures are included.

Previously Listed Apps

These seventeen apps listed here have been discussed elsewhere in this text or in the companion text, *Not a Toy, but a Tool*. Here they are organized in four categories, according to the appropriate level of English language learning: All Levels of Learning, Beginning Level, High Beginning and Intermediate Levels, and High Intermediate and Advanced Levels. Only two apps are listed for the High Intermediate and Advanced Levels. However, at that level, virtually all of the apps listed in both this book and in the companion book can be used to engage the student and promote the understanding of the English language.

Within each of the categories, the apps are listed alphabetically, with information on the exact chapter that includes a more thorough discussion of the app. Because ELL students are primarily concerned with learning English, the majority of the apps are found in chapter 4 of *Not a Toy, but a Tool*. That chapter specifically addresses the study of the English language. However, some apps are listed from other chapters in this book.

Apps Appropriate for All Levels
1. *Edmodo* by Edmodo, Free (also available on Android), chapter 2 of *Not a Toy, but a Tool*—Students can access homework, grades, class discussions, and notifications, as well as video and audio files. The app is perfect for the flipped classroom.
2. *Educreations Interactive Whiteboard* by Educreations, Free, chapter 2 of *Not a Toy, but a Tool*—Users can insert text and graphics, then record directions, and finally save a short video file. The app is perfect for the flipped classroom.

3. *Dictionary.com Dictionary & Thesaurus for iPad* by Dictionary.com, Free, $0.99, or $4.99 (also available on Android), chapter 4 of *Not a Toy, but a Tool*—Several features are invaluable for ELL students. When reading a word, an ELL student can look up the definition. However, a student may not know the meaning of a word from an audio recording. This apps allows students who are unsure of the meaning or spelling of a word to tap on the little microphone that is just to the right of the search box to speak the word. If the word is not correctly pronounced, the app provides possible words that sound similar.

4. *Learn English with busuu!* by Busuu Limited, Free, with additional in-app purchases for $4.99 each (also available on Android), chapter 6 of *Not a Toy, but a Tool*—The app is described on iTunes as providing "comprehensive audio-visual learning material with pictures and recordings by native speakers." Twenty-five units are provided with the free version. The description of this app in the companion book is provided from the perspective of learning French. However, the features are virtually the same with the *Learn English* equivalent.

5. *iPrompt Pro* by OurApps4U Limited, Free, chapter 3 of *Not a Toy, but a Tool*—This app is a virtual teleprompter. Settings can be set very slow, which allows ELL students to practice reading at a slow space. The rate of scrolling can be increased as a student's reading ability increases.

6. *Remind101* by remind101, Free (also available on Android), chapter 5 of this book—Through this app, teachers can set up a system for texting and e-mailing students through cellular phones. Neither teachers nor students can see the phone numbers, but the contacts can be made individually or to groups. Using this app in combination with Google Translate is a terrific way to keep parents informed of classroom activities. Remind101 is also a perfect tool to use with the flipped classroom.

7. *Skitch* by Evernote, Free (also available on Android), chapter 3 of *Not a Toy, but a Tool*—This app is for annotating images. While that is a useful tool for all teachers, ELL students enjoy working with this app. Teachers can assign certain images and students could be asked to label the images and also add words that express the feelings that might be conveyed by the image, thus providing the students with ample practice using their vocabulary.

8. *Skype* by Skype Communications, Free (also available on Android), chapter 3 of *Not a Toy, but a Tool*—The United States is a far larger country than most of the homelands represented by ELL students. Through this app, students can begin to understand the great variety

of cultures and accents within the boundaries of the United States. Skype allows teachers to connect with representatives from various areas of this country. Also docents from famous historic sites could be scheduled to speak to the students, explaining the significance of the sites.

Apps Appropriate for Beginning Level
1. *Abby: Animals Phonics Island Adventure* by 22learn, LLC, Free or $1.99, chapter 4 of *Not a Toy, but a Tool*—This is especially good for elementary students who are at the basic or low-intermediate levels of proficiency. A cute monkey goes on a trip Phonics Island. A variety of activities are available with this app. Each activity provides recordings with the correct phonetic pronunciations.
2. *Cimo Can Spell (Lite)* by PlaySmart-Kids, Free or $2.99, chapter 4 of *Not a Toy, but a Tool*—This adorable app provides opportunities to learn to spell and pronounce words correctly. The words are divided into six levels of difficulty. The designer explains, "Some of the app's 100 words can be sounded out using common phonics rules (i.e., grouped by short vowel, long vowel, Bossy R's and other vowel team words), and others do not follow those normal rules and must be memorized."
3. *Word Wall HD* by Punflay/Emantras, Inc., $1.99, chapter 4 of *Not a Toy, but a Tool*—This is especially good for elementary students who are at the basic or low-intermediate levels of proficiency. As each letter in the *writing abc* area, or word in the *writing words* area is tapped, a recording provides the correct phonetic pronunciation. The user then hears a request to repeat the pronunciation.

Apps Appropriate for High Beginning and Intermediate Level
1. *3rd Grade 4th Grade Life Science Reading Comprehension* by Abitalk Incorporated, Free for four stories; additional sixteen stories for $2.99, chapter 3 of this book—The feature that allows students to tap on any word to hear the correct pronunciation would be tremendous for learners of the English language.
2. *Booksy* by TipiTap, Inc., Free, chapter 4 of *Not a Toy, but a Tool*—Provides opportunity to practice reading, especially appropriate for elementary students at the intermediate level. As a student practices reading, tapping on any individual word that seems difficult elicits a recording of the correct pronunciation.

3. *Dictionary & Thesaurus for iPad* by Dictionary.com, LLC, Free, chapter 4 of *Not a Toy, but a Tool*—This app is a valuable resource for this and higher levels of ELL students.

4. *My Grammar Lab Intermediate* by Pearson Education, Free, chapter 4 of *Not a Toy, but a Tool*—This app teaches the basics of English grammar, and is appropriate for intermediate learners.

Apps Appropriate for High Intermediate and Advanced Level

1. *Free Books: 23,469 Classics to Go* by Digital Press Publishing, Free, $0.99, or $3.99, chapter 4 of *Not a Toy, but a Tool*—These are great books for advanced intermediate and higher levels of ELL students. The collection of books by Mark Twain, as well as several books in the categories of war and Westerns, can teach new immigrants a great deal about the American culture.

2. *Vocabulary for GRE, SAT, ACT, GMAT, IELTS, TOEFL, ESL, English, Language, Education, Words, Word Power, Exercise* by SuVoBi, Free initially, other options $0.99 or $6.99, chapter 4 of *Not a Toy, but a Tool*—This is particularly appropriate for proficient and advanced proficient learners at the high school level.

Additional Highly Rated Apps for English Language Learners

A few other apps are listed here that offer teachers an excellent opportunity to supplement classroom work with another source for teaching basic skills. These apps are highly recommended. Space restrictions for this book prevent a more complete description.

- *U.S.A. Learns: 1st English Course (Units 1–5)* by Sacramento County Office of Education, Free—There are three other free units available, for a total of twenty units.
- *Duolingo,* by Duolingo, Free—Carnegie Mellon University professor Luis von Ahn originally designed this app as a private endeavor. However, the app went public in November of 2012 and has remained both free and highly rated. Aside from five different languages for English speakers, the following sections provide excellent learning activities for ELL students:
  - *Anglais á partir du français:* English for French speakers
  - *Inglês a partir de portugués:* English for Portuguese speakers
  - *Inglés desde español:* English for Spanish speakers
  - *Inglese da italiano:* English for Italian speakers

Reflections on Chapter Six

One area not discussed in this chapter is conversational English. An app that focuses on conversation would be extremely valuable for learners of English, both in the classroom and at home. There are in fact several apps that cover conversational English. However, none could be found that met the requirement of being both highly rated and available for a low cost. The following is just a short list of several apps that might be appropriate for readers to check out. One is too expensive to be included fully in this book and the others have not yet received sufficient ratings.

Recommendations and comments about the following apps are encouraged through the wiki associated with the author's two iPad books. The address and access directions are described in the introduction of this book.

- *Conversation English HD* by The English App, $2.99—Cost knocked this one out of being described further, although it is fairly highly rated.
- *Common Conversations* (*Daily Listening Conversation, Easy English for Beginners*) by Dien Le, Free—Includes about one hundred practical conversations.
- *English Conversation* by Vu Truong Thanh, Free—Promises to provide 1,700 conversations on forty different topics.

Whether teaching conversation, grammar, reading, or facts about specific subjects, all teachers know that every classroom has its own unique characteristics. Just as every student is different, so every classroom reflects a particular climate and culture. That uniqueness is exaggerated with ELL classrooms, as the differences are not only based on the personalities, but also on the languages and cultures of the students.

Learning to teach well in a classroom with such diverse learners requires skill and patience. Over forty apps have been mentioned in this chapter. Each app addresses a different need, but, used well, they can each facilitate a great deal of learning that might otherwise not be so easily achieved.

CHAPTER SEVEN

———*ᘯᘯᘯ*———

Teaching Special Needs Students with the iPad

A vast range of categories exist under the umbrella of *special needs*, and an entire book could easily be dedicated solely to apps for these students. There are students with learning disabilities, as well as students who are gifted. Some students have been diagnosed with attention-deficit hyperactivity disorder (ADHD), while others struggle with speech impediments. Then there are autistic students, as well as students with Down syndrome. Other students have visual or hearing losses. The categories seem to have no end and the task of limiting the selection of apps to a number manageable within a single chapter creates quite a dilemma.

In all, eight different categories of special education are addressed in this chapter. Because of the differences in needs for each category, the discussions vary significantly from one section to the next. Most sections have brief discussions of apps that have been more thoroughly discussed in either other chapters of this book or in the companion book *Not a Toy, but a Tool*.

Interspersed among the brief discussions, six new apps are presented with a more complete discussion. Then, often at the end of each category, a list is provided of additional highly rated apps that can have significant value for a student who has that specific need. Following are the eight categories of special needs addressed in this chapter, presented in alphabetical order:

- ADHD
- Auditory impairments
- Autism

- Down syndrome
- Dyscalculia, dyslexia, and learning disabilities
- Gifted
- Speech and language impairments
- Visual impairments

—⁊⁊⁊—

Attention Deficit Hyperactivity Disorder

Focus GPS Lite
Developer: Memory on Demand, LLC
Website: www.memory-on-demand.com/
Cost: Free or $4.99 for Pro app

In early 2012, the designers announced that this app was "designed to en-hance the memory, concentration, and organizational capabilities of children and adults with ADHD" (PRWeb). That certainly addresses the specific needs of ADHD. However, it has been included here with some reservations, based on two concerns: (1) Other than one brief video, there appears to be little documentation; and (2) the free prices seem only to apply to a thirty-day trial. Teachers should evaluate whether the price is worth the investment.

No other app seems to be specifically designed for ADHD's specific needs. At the bottom of the introductory screen for this app, the designer includes the expression "Apps for Organizing & Prioritizing." The average ADHD student frequently struggles with procrastination, organization, and the or-deal of prioritizing. This app goes a long way with addressing those problems. The intended users include both students and adults. The second screen lists the following seven links that are also always available from the menu at the bottom of the screen:

- Getting Started
- File Management
- New Thought (Create a New Thought-Line)
- View Entries
- What's Up?
- Search All Entries

The Getting Started area provides a YouTube video that explains the main features of the app. That website is also provided online (www.youtube.com/watch?v=75BsukuTMbA), so that new users can watch the video from

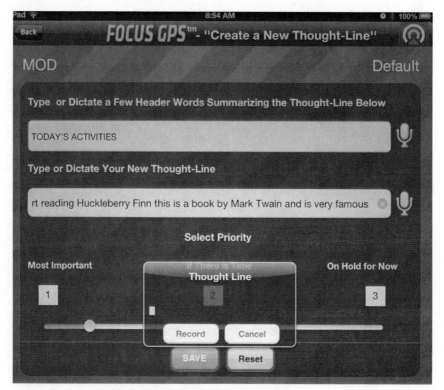

Figure 7.1. Focus CPS: Thought-line Area.
Image created by the author.

their laptop, while proceeding through the steps on the iPad. The best place to start is with "Create a New Thought-Line," which opens a screen with an area to type or dictate a few headers or title words, as well as an area to type or dictate a new "Thought-line," as shown in figure 7.1.

The speech-to-text feature is extremely valuable for an ADHD student. This feature has been shown to provide much better accuracy than many speech-to-text apps. To record, first tap on the microphone image on the right. Then a small window appears, as shown near the bottom of figure 7.1. Tap the *Record* button and, before beginning to speak, listen for the recording to state that it is "listening." The recording automatically stops as soon as there is a pause in the user's voice. At the bottom of the screen, a priority setting can be made. After the user taps the green *Save* button, the file is placed in the *Entries* area of the app.

In the *Entries* area, each item is listed with the most recent at top, and the associated priorities at the left. However, tapping on the title at the top of each column changes the order from ascending to descending order. That feature is particularly valuable for the priority column, as those that were rated as "most important" can be grouped together at the top.

The *What's Up* area provides a great way to organize the day's activities. On the right side are buttons to sort by *What's Up* and *What's Done*. In addition, there is a button to share by printing or through e-mail. Two areas remain. The *Search All Entries* area allows the user to search for a specific entry. Finally, the *File Management* area provides another way to manage different files. A few other features are available, but the basics provide a great way to start. Making incremental steps toward improving organization can boost a student's confidence considerably.

Additional Highly Rated App for ADHD Students

1. *Social Skills Sampler HD* by The Conover Company, Free—The focus of this app is on allowing a student to adapt behavior to acquire lifelong social skills. Videos are included for the following categories: Meeting/Greeting, Take Responsibility, Be Polite and Courteous, Join Others in Groups, Apologize/Express Self, Follow Directions, and Handle Criticism. Each video shows sample behavior with periodic stops, so a student and his or her teacher can discuss the main points. This designer has produced four dozen different apps for use by special needs students. Following are five apps that show particular relevance for the ADHD student. Each costs $1.99.
   o *Everyday Social Skills HD*
   o *Communication Skills HD*
   o *Responding Social Skills HD*
   o *Manners HD*
   o *Safety Signs & Words HD*

Auditory Impairments

The following three apps have been discussed more fully in *Not a Toy, but a Tool,* but are also included here because they have significant value for a student with auditory disabilities.

1. *Dragon Dictation* by Nuance Communication, Free (also available on Android), Discussed fully in *Not a Toy, but a Tool,* chapter 3—When the user begins talking and provides punctuation as needed, the recording converts the spoken words to text that can then be read easily by a

hearing-impaired student. The postings also can be e-mailed to teachers or posted elsewhere.

2. *Learn American Sign Language* by Selectsoft, $1.99 (also available on Android), discussed fully in *Not a Toy, but a Tool*, chapter 6—The primary purpose is for learning sign language. Each chapter has a video of professional sign language interpreter Renee Moore explaining the various signs.

3. *Baby Sign and Learn* by Baby Sign and Learn, Free or $2.99 (also available on Android), discussed fully in *Not a Toy, but a Tool*, chapter 6—With adorable graphics, this app serves as an introduction to sign language for PK or K learners. The free app only comes with only ten words, whereas the paid version includes over three hundred words.

Autism Spectrum Disorder

Most of the valuable apps that address autism spectrum disorder (ASD) come with a high price tag. A few low-cost apps are briefly discussed here, although most apps in this category cost much more than the $1.99 limit normally maintained in this book. Regardless, each of the apps has significant value.

1. *Autism Tracker Lite: Track, analyze and share ASD daily* by Track & Share APPS, LLC, Free or $9.99 for Autism Tracker Pro—The opening screen shares the title *Autism Tracker*, along with the statement "track what matters, gain insights, collaborate." This app provides a valuable tool for teachers of autistic children, as well as any child who has behavior disorders. The primary purpose is to record and follow behavior of a student on a daily basis to learn trends and share information with parents or other professionals.

2. *AutisMate* by SpecialNeedsWare, Free or $149.99—On iTunes, the designer for this app writes, "AutisMate's comprehensive approach encourages the user to develop communication and behavioral skills simultaneously, allowing each skill to build on the other."

3. *Social Stories Creator and Library for Preschool, Autism and Special Needs* by Touch Autism, Free—This app comes with one nine-page story titled *Taking Care of My Device Social Story*. After the story is selected, the screen appears to offer four options: Story, Rules Chart, Read to Me, and Read Myself. The last two are actually options for having the first two played with recordings or silently. The Rules Chart summarizes six rules that are explained in the story. The app also allows

teachers to create an additional story with areas to add images, audio, and text. In addition, nine other stories are available, each for a price ranging from $0.99 to $2.99.

4. *VAST Autism 1—Core* by SpeakinMotion, $4.99—The iTunes store writes that this app "combines the highly effective concept of video modeling with written words and auditory cues to help individuals acquire relevant words, phrases and sentences so that they can speak for themselves." A collection of videos are included, as well as a mirror feature that allows a student to have visual feedback while practicing sounds.

5. *Proloquo2Go* by AssistiveWare, $219.99—Without a doubt, this is the most expensive app mentioned in this book and apparently there is no associated free version. According to the designer, this app "enables people to talk using symbols or typed text in a natural-sounding voice that suits their age and character."

Down Syndrome

Research has shown that students with Down syndrome have difficulty remaining focused during extended periods of direct instructions. Apps are appropriate and extremely effective for breaking the routine, yet still providing a structured environment for learning. Many apps already listed in this book offer a great deal for a student with Down syndrome. The following are four important areas to consider when working with a special needs student:

1. Speech therapy: Each of the apps in the *Speech and Language Impairments* section of this chapter are especially appropriate for addressing the speech difficulties of a student with Down syndrome. Check out both the apps that are fully discussed there.

2. Reading and spelling: For developing spelling and reading skills, all of the apps listed in the elementary section of chapter 4 of *Not a Toy, but a Tool* are appropriate for inclusion here. Especially engaging are the *Cimo Can Spell* and the *Booksy* apps.

3. Mathematics: For working with mathematical skills, the apps described and listed in chapter 2 of this book are all appropriate.

4. Art and music: A fascinating presentation was made at a conference in Chicago in July of 2005, co-sponsored by the National Down Syndrome Society and the National Association for Down Syndrome. A subsequent article was published titled "If People with Down Syndrome Ruled the World." That article includes the statement, "Art

and Music appreciation would be big" (McGuire, 2005). So for the benefit of these students, both art and music should be incorporated into instruction whenever possible. Chapter 4 of this book describes ample apps to meet that need.

Dyscalculia, Dyslexia and Learning Disabilities

Students with dyscalculia (difficulty understanding arithmetic relationships), dyslexia (difficulty with learning to read), and other learning disabilities often suffer from low self-esteem and limited confidence. Apps can help to alleviate those feelings and help to create a more fun and pleasurable environment for learning. The first app fully described here addresses the needs of a student with dyscalculia. Four additional apps follow. All five apps are appropriate for students with various levels of learning disabilities.

—⁓⁓—

Park Math—by Duck Duck Moose
Developer: Duck Duck Moose, Inc.
Website: www.duckduckmoose.com
Cost: $1.99

This award-winning app provides three levels of mathematical skills, based on Common Core standards for kindergarten and first grade. The following skills are covered with each level:

- Level 1: Counting to 20, addition and subtraction with numbers up to 5
- Level 2: Counting to 50, addition and subtraction with numbers up to 10
- Level 3: counting to 100, addition and subtraction with numbers up to 20

The opening screen shows two ducks and then a moose, as a recording plays the name of the designer, "Duck Duck Moose." After that the *Welcome* screen shows a blue bear on roller skates, along with a smaller bear, a dog, a ball, and several other items. Each one of those items move when touched. The bear, however, is the item that explains the different features as the user moves through the app. Whenever the bear is tapped, it skates on to the next screen.

After the Welcome screen, the bear comes to a playground with a swing and a purple rabbit. When the rabbit is tapped, it hops up on the swing and begins to swing back and forth as a recording counts the number of swings.

The counting varies according to the selected level. Throughout the app, the orange kite in the top left corner serves as a way to select a specific activity without having to proceed consecutively through the activities. The yellow kite is the same as the second activity, which focuses on adding single or double digits.

Figure 7.2 shows that second activity at the third level. For all levels, a problem is shown at the top. The number of ducks shown on the top of the play equipment corresponds to the top addend of the problem, whereas the number of ducks waiting on the grass corresponds to the second number. The possible answers are shown on the top right and the numerical representation of the problem is shown below the possible answers.

The user should be encouraged to determine the answer first, but wait to tap on the answer. Instead the student can first check his or her answer by tapping on each duck in the grass. After each tapped duck climbs to the top, along with the other ducks, the succeeding number is shown on its breast. When the final duck reaches the top, the final number represents the answer.

In figure 7.2, the first duck is in the process of climbing up the ladder. A student can also tap on the ducks that are already on the top. They appear to

Figure 7.2. Math Park: Addition at the Third Level.
Image created by the author.

briefly dance a bit. When all the ducks are on top, the student can then tap on the correct answer. The bear applauds for a correct answer, as each duck slides down the large red slide, on the right. If the wrong answer is selected, the bear simply shakes his head to indicate "No," so the student can continue on to make another selection.

The following five activities are also associated with this app:

- Greater than/less than concepts are explained by asking the student to balance a seesaw by adding and subtracting mice.
- Subtraction is covered by friendly apples that fall from a tree.
- Sorting is covered by asking the student to arrange dogs in order of the numbers that appear on their purple shirts.
- Patterns are taught through an activity in which the student needs to move an item to complete a pattern.
- Counting is a requirement of the last activity, which requires the student to feed a purple hippo a specified number of items.

Having fun is an integral part of every activity with this app; every animal and many other objects move in some way when touched. Furthermore, the student is praised for correct answers. Learning becomes a positive experience when working with apps such as *Park Math*. The following apps are all designed to engage, as well as promote learning.

Previously Discussed Apps for Learning Disabilities

The following apps address the problems associated with dyscalculia, dyslexia, or other learning disabilities, and are discussed more fully elsewhere:

1. Mathematics and dyscalculia issues were discussed previously. The following are two other apps that address the issues of learning disability in this area.
   a. *Calculator for iPad Free* by International Travel Weather Calculator, chapter 2 of this book, Free or $1.99—In the App store, typing in the word "calculator" brings up a plethora of calculator apps, many highly rated. However, as explained in chapter 2, while the device is held horizontally, this app has some advanced features. In the vertical position, this apps provides all the basics necessary for arithmetic calculations, without the intimidating features used in advanced math classes.
   b. *Algebra Touch* by Regular Berry Software, LLC, $2.99—As fully discussed in chapter 2 of this book, this app is well worth the

investment for all children. For learning-disabled children, it has tremendous value in adding interactive features that assist with the understanding of key algebraic concepts.

2. Spelling can be a real challenge for a student with dyslexia and other learning disabilities. Keep it fun with apps like these:
   a. *Cimo Can Spell (Lite)* by PlaySmart-Kids, Free or $2.99—Described fully in chapter 4 of *Not a Toy, but a Tool.*
   b. *First Words Sampler* by Learning Touch, Free—The emphasis is on letters, sounds, and spelling. This is an excellent starter app for young children.

3. Reading can be one of the most frustrating areas for a student with dyslexia and other learning disabilities. *Booksy: Learn to Read Platform* by Tipitap Inc. (also available on Android) brings the word *fun* into the process of reading. Three books are provided free with additional books for $0.99 each. This app is described fully in chapter 4 of *Not a Toy, but a Tool.*

Additional Highly Rated Apps for Dyslexic and Learning-Disabled Students

Both the following apps have outstanding features that address the reading difficulties of special needs students.

1. *Meet Heckerty: A funny interactive family storybook for learning to read* by Broomstick Productions, Inc., Free (also available on Android)—This app tells the amusing story of a 409-year-old, green-faced witch. Effective animations are included.

2. *Dr. Seuss Bookcase* by Oceanhouse Media, Free for specific sections of each book—This app opens with a bookcase chock full of Dr. Seuss books. Although not entirely free, the books do provide stellar opportunities for engaging a student with significant learning opportunities. This app is appropriate for all students, but is particularly valuable for a student with a learning disability. The free books are only samplers; paid books vary in price from $0.99 to $3.99 each. Each book offers three selections: Read to Me, Read it Myself, and Auto Play. In addition, tapping on any figure or object within a page brings up the name of the object, with a recording of the name. A menu is accessible from the lower left corner, which includes a settings area for making several adjustments.

Gifted

The National Association of Gifted Children has long recognized the importance of challenging gifted children sufficiently to avoid the boredom that stems from the repetitive nature of typical class lessons. The iPad is an outstanding tool for providing a gifted student with supplemental and challenging apps that can keep them engaged and learning, while the rest of the class participates in activities that gifted student might deem to be tedious.

The one app fully described here exemplifies the type of app that provides additional challenges for the gifted student, but might simply be seen as frustrating to a regular student. Several other apps are also listed. All the apps in this section were chosen for their ability to include one or more of the following three features:

- Supplemental instructional material
- Greater depth on material being covered by the class
- Additional training for higher level courses, such as for AP coursework

—*osso*—

Minds of Modern Mathematics
Recommended Grade Levels: 9–12
Developer: IBM Corp.
Website: mindsofmath.com
Cost: Free

This app provides an interactive history of mathematics from 1000 to 1950. iTunes states that this story of mathematics has "impacted almost every aspect of human progress, from science to music, art, architecture, and culture." A student who is gifted in the area of mathematics would likely be intrigued and challenged with this app, learning more than the basics of mathematics. The information also easily allows cross-curriculum studies.

The opening screen provides information about the 1964 World's Fair exhibit that served as the inspiration for this app. Swiping to the left brings up a screen shown in figure 7.3. Arrows and labels have been added to each of the nine menu items. Tapping on the small *i* on the lower menu returns the user to the opening information screen. By default, the second screen is on the *Century* setting on the top menu.

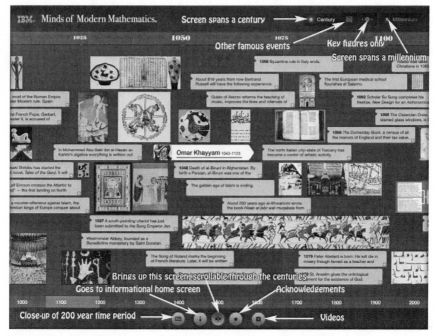

Figure 7.3. Timeline Screen with Instructional Information Added.
Image created by the author.

The names of mathematicians are always written in the white areas. Tapping on a name brings up a screen that has an image of the mathematician, as well as three paragraphs about his or her accomplishments. Links are also provided to websites that have more thorough information. Once on the website, a *Return* button is provided to return to the app. Underneath the image may be one or more thumbnails of other images associated with the mathematician. To return to the timeline, users simply tap on the X provided on the right side, above the descriptions.

Each blue area on the main timeline brings up a small window describing an event that occurred during a specific year. Tapping on other areas brings up an image with a brief description to the right. Both the green areas and all the thumbnail images on the timeline access large images with descriptions in a format the same as those shown with individual mathematicians. The last icon on the lower menu accesses six powerful videos. The gifted student is usually mesmerized by those videos, each on different mathematical topics.

Two other areas can be linked from the two center icons on the top menu. Just to the right of the *Century* icon is a link that brings up another timeline directly above the main timeline. The names of famous historical individuals and events are included in this area, so the student can understand the culture in which the mathematicians were living. Tapping just to the left of the *Millennium* link brings up a timeline with the names of mathematicians only.

A gifted student can have a heyday with this app, making discoveries, writing reports, or re-proving mathematical theorems. One student might enjoy looking into Fibonacci's proof that $x^3 + 2x^2 + 10x = 20$ cannot be solved by square roots. As an example of another project, a teacher might provide a student with a pipe and a source of water and ask the student to discover the relationship between the speed of liquid flow with the cross-section of the pipe. That relationship was demonstrated first by Leonardo da Vinci.

Additional Highly Rated Apps for the Gifted Student

1. *GeoBee Challenge HD* by National Geographic Society, $1.99, recommended grade levels: 5–8—Database includes over 1300 questions and an interactive map to access over one thousand different locations. A fun challenge is to find the location of an unidentified photograph.
2. *Smithsonian Channel App* by Smithsonian Networks, Free (also available on Android), recommended grade levels: 9–12—Includes hundreds of video clips and full episodes. A student can search for videos and also save a favorites listing.
3. Most AP apps are above the cost limits set for inclusion in this book. However, the following two apps are both free:
   ○ *AP Exam Prep—Calculus* by gWhiz, LCC, Free (also available on Android)
   ○ *AP Biology Hardy-Weinberg Spreadsheet Tutorial* by Quantum Technology, Inc., Free

Previously Discussed Apps for Gifted Student

PrepZilla—Study with Your Friends Test Prep Game by gWhiz, LLC, Free or additional features for fees—This app is described in chapter 2 of this book. Topics include AP calculus and AP statistics.

Speech and Language Impairments

Having a speech disorder usually severely affects a child's relationship with both teachers and peers. The frequency of speech impediments is much higher with young children, but if not addressed can lead to severe depression and an inability to function effectively in life. In September 2010, the National Institute on Deafness and Other Communication Disorders reported that 8–9 percent of young children have been diagnosed with speech disorders, dropping to 5 percent as they enter first grade. This is obviously a major problem and the apps in this section can significantly assist teachers and students with addressing speech problems.

The following two apps each provide significant help with speech therapy. However, the iPad lends itself to being able to help in this area. Readers are encouraged to check the apps listed in the *Additional Highly Rated Apps* section.

⟶⟶⟶

Speech with Milo: Interactive Storybook
Developer: Doonan Speech Therapy
Website: www.speechwithmilo.com/
Cost: $1.99
Addresses: Speech therapy

The designer of this app is a licensed speech therapist. The app website shows that he has created eight different *Speech with Milo* apps. Each addresses speech therapy and most, including this one, are highly rated. This *Interactive Storybook* app is the least expensive, with six being priced at $2.99. *Speech with Milo Pro* bears a price of $23.99.

The home screen shows four different buttons: *Instructions, Go, Settings,* and *Table of Contents*. The *Instructions* area provides fairly complete instructions, explaining that the student can improve their language skills by telling their own stories. Recordings of each student then become part of an interactive storybook.

The *Settings* area has four toggle switches and six buttons:

- Background Sound: toggle switch
- Listen to Narrator: toggle switch
- Text: toggle switch (this refers to statements that appear on each page)
- Interactive Features: toggle switch
- Home: returns user to the home screen
- Instructions: links to the Instructions area, described previously
- Therapy Ideas: requires Internet access
- Sign up for our Newsletter: requires first and last name and e-mail address
- Tell a Friend: sends an e-mail with a built-in link to the iTunes page for this app
- Send us Feedback: also in an e-mail format

Figure 7.4.   Speech with Milo: Story Telling Screen.
Image created by the author.

Table of Contents is the third button on the homepage and it links to a page that lists thirty-three different topics that all relate to Milo. The topics can serve as the storyline associated with each picture. For example, selecting "Milo on the Swing" brings up the image shown in figure 7.4. As a student taps on the *Listen* button in the lower left, a recording plays the sentence written at the top.

If a teacher wishes to have a student strengthen listening skills, the settings area toggle switch can be set so that no text appears on the various topic pages. Each page comes with a *record* button, a red circle located in the upper right area of the screen. The student can tap on the circle to begin and end a recording. The button to the right of the record button is the playback button. Each image also has interactive features. For the image shown in figure 7.4, the squirrel's tail moves, the soccer ball spins, the ladybug changes colors, the flamingo moves, a little mouse pops out the balloon's basket, and Milo says his name.

This app does an excellent job at promoting creativity. Students enjoy this app and teachers can use it to effective promote better speech quality.

—ᴡᴡ—

Phonics Genius
Developer: Innovative Mobile Apps
Website: www.alligatorapps.com/
Cost: Free
Addresses: Speech therapy with phonics, for students who have some previous experience with reading

This app provides a student with both studying and gaming options. The opening screen, shown in figure 7.5, has twenty different letter groupings, listed alphabetically. Over twelve different screens, the app provides a total of 226 different groups of letters for a student to practice reading. The groupings vary from only one letter to as many as five letters. Each grouping has a selection of cards to read and record.

For example, the white card area with *ai* brings up the word *mermaid* with the letters *ai* in red and a recording provides the correct pronunciation. At the bottom left corner is a *Record* button, which allows a student to make a recording as he or she tries to correctly pronounce the word. The recordings can be played back for the teacher to check the accuracy of the pronunciation. A student can also overwrite first attempts with a new recording, as improvements are made in acquiring correct diction.

The designer has provided over six thousand words within this app. Each time a specific category is selected, a new word is provided, which offers additional experience. As each word appears, a star is shown on the menu bar. Tapping on the star allows the word to be moved to a favorites area that can be used for later study. A speaker is also provided to adjust the volume. On the last screen of the app, a large yellow star opens an area where all the student's favorite words have been saved. Next to the star is the *Shuffle* icon.

Two extremely important icons are available from the top menu bar of the home screen. The information icon explains all the different features provided within this one app, including the gaming features. For the student who individually owns or operates the iPad, instructions are also provided for personalizing the app in a variety of ways, such as adding or editing specific cards or entire categories.

Five different games can be accessed, in which the student hears a word and then they must select the corresponding written word. The settings area allows users to set the selection to a group of two, three, four, five, or six

Figure 7.5. Phonics Genius Home Screen.
Image created by the author.

words. If the correct word is selected, the student hears a recording of "Well done!" The recording for incorrect answers is "That's not right" and then the student is allowed to try another selection. This app offers much more than might seem evident from the home screen.

Additional Highly Rated Apps for Students with Speech and Language Impairments

1. *Farm Academy* by Virtual Speech Center, Inc., $0.99—This app was created for young children (eighteen months–three years) by a certified speech and language pathologist. Both a *Play and Learn* area, children can identify specific animals, an assortment of foods, and various sizes. Additionally young students can practice counting.

2. *Language TherAppy Lite* by Tactis Therapy Solutions, Ltd., Free or $59.99 for the full version—On iTunes, the designer describes this as a "complete speech therapy toolkit." Altogether the designer has developed ten different apps that address different areas of special needs children, although the emphasis is on language development.

3. *SpeechBox for Speech Therapy (Apraxia, Autism, Down's Syndrome)* by the Jonah Bonah Learning Company, $19.99—This is costly, but the only negative comment on iTunes was about the cost. It is highly rated and does specifically address the need for speech therapy.

   ○ Virtualspeechcenter.com (www.virtualspeechcenter.com/Mobile Apps.aspx) lists twenty-two other apps that have value for working with speech therapy. Many of them were designed by certified speech and language pathologists.

Visual Impairments

The most powerful feature of the iPad for visually impaired students is the VoiceOver feature. This hidden feature that has tremendous value. To learn how to activate the feature, visit Apple's support website: support.apple.com/kb/ht4064.

After VoiceOver has been activated, every action on the iPad will play a recording, so even without any sight, the user can use apps. With this feature on, the user needs to realize that all gestures are different. Instead of the single tap to open apps and areas of apps, the user must use a double tab. Scrolling is accomplished with three fingers. A list of VoiceOver gestures is included on p. 103 of the iPad User Guide: manuals.info.apple.com/MANUALS/1000/MA1595/en_US/ipad_user_guide.pdf.

VoiceOver works with all the built-in apps of the iPad. Unfortunately, not all apps are able to utilize the VoiceOver feature. Both of the apps listed here do come with VoiceOver, as well as the others in the *Additional Highly Rated Apps* section.

—⁓—

Color ID Free
Developer: GreenGar Studios
Website: www.greengar.com/
Cost: Free
Addresses: Color identification for the visually impaired, including color blind

This app has the amazing ability to share with a visually impaired person the color of any specific object. The operation is as simple as opening the app and holding the rear-facing camera in front of an object. A recording immediately names the color and continues to share the colors as the iPad is moved. For the color blind, the advantage is obvious. However, even individuals who have complete loss of sight can learn to use the app. If the person learns the location of the app, he or she simply needs to tap and open the app. The app immediately begins to share colors.

For those with sight, some additional features are available. The name of the color is written on the top of the screen. The icon of two squares on the top right serves as a toggle switch between exotic and simple colors. For most situations, the basic colors provide the most useful setting.

A camera icon on the right takes a picture and then brings up a menu with the following five options:

- The first icon on the left allows the image to be saved to the Photos area where it can be retrieved at any time.
- An envelope icon brings up an e-mail, with the image attached and ready to be sent to a recipient.
- The F icon posts the image to Facebook.
- The T icon connects to Twitter.
- The X icon simply closes that menu.

The icon on the bottom right allows the user to switch between the forward and rear-facing camera. The icon in the lower right corner can stop the recordings from reading colors, which is useful to use until the camera is in position.

Previously Discussed App for Students with Visual Impairments
1. *Evernote* by Evernote, Free, *Not a Toy, but a Tool*, chapter 2—For storing text, notes and photographs. The app comes with VoiceOver support. Notes can be recorded, rather than typed.
2. *Dragon Dictation* by Nuance Communication, Free, *Not a Toy, but a Tool*, chapter 3—The app comes with VoiceOver support. After speaking words and any needed punctuation, the spoken words are converted to text that can then be sent or posted elsewhere.
3. *Booksy, Not a Toy, but a Tool*, chapter 4—This app has books appropriate for elementary age children. The *Listen* feature can be activated to assist a visually impaired student.

Additional Highly Rated Apps for the Visually Impaired Student
1. *Light Detector* by EveryWare Technologies, Free—This app simply emits a sound that increases in volume with a closer proximity to light.
2. *VM Alert—Video Motion Detector* by Adam Uccello, $1.99—This app is a pure and simple motion detector.
3. *VisionSim* by Evil Genius Technologies, Free—This app is not so much for the visually impaired as it is for a teacher to provide a sighted student with an understanding of the world as seen through the eyes of a student who is suffering from macular degeneration, diabetic retinopathy, glaucoma, or cataracts. With increased understanding, the student usually displays greater empathy for the visually impaired.
4. *Magnifying Glass with Light: Digital magnifier with flashlight* by Falcon in Motion, LLC, Free, although Pro version is $1.99—Allows any text to be magnified with light that automatically comes on in low light. A stabilizer and other features are available with the Pro version. This can help a student with low vision tremendously. It also comes with VoiceOver features.

Reflections on Chapter 7

As mentioned in the opening paragraph of this chapter, special education addresses a tremendous range of needs. One textbook describes special education as "individualized education and services for students with disabilities" (Smith & Tyler, 2009). By its very nature, the iPad was designed to offer "individualized education," thus offering significant value to the special education classroom.

iPads were never intended to be shared, but rather to be owned by a single user and adapted for that individual's needs. About three dozen apps have been discussed in this chapter, covering eight major categories of special education. Each app, appropriately chosen for a specific need, can contribute significantly to creating greater understanding for a special needs student.

References

Barseghian, T. (2012, January 23). Study Shows Algebra iPad App Improves Scores in One School. Mind/Shift. How We Learn. Retrieved from blogs.kqed.org/mindshift/2012/01/study-shows-algebra-ipad-app-improves-scores-in-one-school/.

Bloomberg Businessweek. (2010, May 18). Viewpoint: What chief executives really want. Retrieved from www.businessweek.com/innovate/content/may2010/id20100517_190221.htm.

Bonnington, C. (2012, January 23). iPad a solid education tool, student reports, WIRED. Retrieved from www.cnn.com/2012/01/23/tech/innovation/ipad-solid-education-tool/index.html.

Brandweiner, N. (2013, June 6). Understand, engage, deliver: Which is most critical for customer retention? Retrieved from www.mycustomer.com/news/understand-engage-deliver-which-most-critical-customer-retention.

Castle, S. (n.d.). Benefits of youth sports, Kids Play Foundation. Retrieved from kidsplayusafoundation.org/benefits-of-youth-sports.

Cutraro, J. (2013). How creativity powers science, Student Science. Retrieved from student.societyforscience.org/article/how-creativity-powers-science.

Einstein, A. (n.d.). Albert Einstein quotes on education. Retrieved from www.fanpop.com/clubs/quotes/articles/80874/title/albert-einstein-quotes-on-education.

Elgan, M. (2010, April 17). Why the iPad is a creativity machine. Computerworld. Retrieved from www.computerworld.com/s/article/9175687/Why_the_iPad_is_a_creativity_machine.

Faas, R. (2012, August 16). How the iPad is transforming the classroom, Cult of Mac. Retrieved from www.cultofmac.com/185048/how-the-ipad-is-transforming-the-classroom-back-to-school/.

Fisher, D., and Frey, N. (2007). *Checking for understanding: Formative assessment techniques for your classroom*. Alexandria, VA: Association for Supervision and Curriculum Development.

Gorman, S. (2012, December 19). U.S. teen smoking declines to record low in 2012—study. *Chicago Tribune*, Business. Retrieved from articles.chicagotribune .com/2012-12-19/business/sns-rt-usa-smokingyouthl1e8njlj9-20121219_1_ dissolvable-products-cigarette-taxes-eighth-graders.

Hoffman, P. (2012, November 28). Science360 (for iPad). *PC Magazine*. Retrieved from www.pcmag.com/article2/0,2817,2412557,00.asp.

Hwang, S. (2012, April 2). iPads in K12 classrooms—empowering students but furthering the learning gap. Retrieved from blog.lib.umn.edu/tel/blog/2012/04/ ipads-in-k12-classrooms---empo.html.

Jennings, G. (2012, February 13). Excellent Academic Results with Trinity's iPad Pilot Group. Retrieved from ipadpilot.wordpress.com/2012/02/13/excellent -academic-results-with-trinitys-ipad-pilot-group/.

Klowsowski, T. (2012, April 12). Your iPad: The creative tool you never knew you needed. *Lifehacker.com*. Retrieved from lifehacker.com/5901341/your-ipad-the -creative-tool-you-never-knew-you-needed.

Mayo Clinic (2011). Nutrition and healthy eating. Retrieved from www.mayoclinic .com/health/water/NU00283/NSECTIONGROUP=2.

McGuire, D. (2005) If people with Down syndrome ruled the world, *National Association for Down Syndrome*. Retrieved from www.nads.org/pages_new/news/ ruletheworld.html.

McIntyre, B. (2012, August 3). Peyton Manning embraces Broncos iPad playbook, *NFL.com*. Retrieved from www.nfl.com/news/story/09000d5d82a5cafe/article/ peyton-manning-embraces-broncos-ipad-playbook?campaign=Twitter_atl.

Meyer, D. (2010, March). Dan Meyer: Math class needs a makeover. Video retrieved from www.ted.com/talks/dan_meyer_math_curriculum_makeover.html.

National Association for Gifted Children (2009, January 15). Creativity: An Essential Element in Your Mathematics Classroom. Retrieved from www.education .com/reference/article/Ref_Creativity_Essential/.

National Institute on Deafness and Other Communication Disorders (NIDCD). (2010, September). NIDCD fact sheet, speech and language developmental milestones. Retrieved from www.nidcd.nih.gov/staticresources/health/voice/speech languagedevelopmentalmilestonesenglishfs.pdf.

Ogden, C.L., Carroll, M.D., Kit, B.K., and Flegal, K.M. (2012, February 1). Prevalence of Obesity and Trends in Body Mass Index Among US Children and Adolescents, 1999–2010. The Journal of the American Medical Association. Retrieved from jama.jamanetwork.com/article.aspx?articleid=1104932.

Partnership for 21st Century Skills. (2011). A framework for 21st century learning. Retrieved from www.p21.org/.

Putnam City Schools. (2013). iPads for student learning, Putnam (Oklahoma) City Schools. Retrieved from www.putnamcityschools.org/District/Bonds/2013 BondElection/iPadsforStudentLearning.aspx.

PRNewswire. (2013, May 29). 2 million IELTS tests in the last year . . . and still growing! *PRNewswire*. Retrieved from www.prnewswire.com/news-releases/2 -million-ielts-tests-in-the-last-year-and-still-growing-209357461.html.

PRWeb. (2012, February 27). Focus GPS (TM), A new Apple iPad app designed to boost academic and cognitive performance of children and adults with ADHD. Retrieved from www.prweb.com/releases/focus-gps/adhd/prweb9228880.htm.

Riconscente, M. (2012). Mobile Learning Game Improves 5th Graders' Fractions Knowledge and Attitudes. Retrieved from www.gamedesk.org/projects/motion -math-in-class/.

Shepherd, I., and Reeves, B. (2011, March 1). iPad or iFad—The reality of a paper-less classroom. Abilene Christian University Mobility Conference. Retrieved from www.acu.edu/technology/mobilelearning/documents/research/ipad-or-ifad.pdf.

Smith, D., and Tyler, N. (2009, January 23). *Introduction to Special Education*. New York: Merrill/Pearson Education.

Stevens, K. (2011, February 4). Using the iPad in ESL learning, language acquisition and portability, *Yahoo! Voices*. Retrieved from voices.yahoo.com/using-ipad-esl -learning-7673184.html.

Strauss, V. (2012, August 24). What to do—and not do—for growing number of English Language Learners. *Washington Post*. Retrieved from www.washingtonpost .com/blogs/answer-sheet/post/what-to-do--and-not-do--for-growing-number-of -english-language-learners/2012/08/23/a1b45c0a-ed81-11e1-a80b-9f898562d010_ blog.html.

T-Ball USA Association. (2014). What is tee ball? T-Ball USA Association. Re-trieved from www.teeballusa.org/What_is_TBall.asp.

TEDx Talks Director. (2007, January 6). Sir Ken Robinson: Do schools kills creativ-ity? Retrieved from www.youtube.com/watch?v=iG9CE55wbtY.

———. (2010, May 13) Dan Meyer: Math class needs a makeover. Retrieved from www.youtube.com/watch?v=NWUFjb8w9Ps.TGfU.

———. (n.d.). Teaching and coaching games for understanding. *TGfU Home*. Re-trieved from tgfuinfo.weebly.com/.

Van Doren, M. (1944). *Liberal education*. New York: Henry Holt and Co.

Wainer, H., and Lysen, S. (2009, July–August). That's funny. . . . A window on data can be a window on discovery. *American Scientist*, 97(4), 272. Retrieved from www.americanscientist.org/issues/pub/thats-funny.

Wilson, J. L. (2013, Oct 25, Creativity Section, p. 6). The 100 Best iPad Apps— Creativity Apps. Retrieved from www.pcmag.com/article2/0,2817,2362577,00.asp.

Index

This index is primarily restricted to all apps that are included in this book, even if the app is just briefly mentioned.

—◦◦◦—

About the Author

Dr. Carrie Thornthwaite is a professor of education at Lipscomb University, in Nashville, TN. In
1997, as she interviewed for the position of Director of Educational Technology, she was asked the
questions, "Are you comfortable with technology?"
With her resounding affirmative response, she was
hired and has been working ever since to promote
the use of technology throughout the education
programs.

Her "comfort" with technology began at a large
insurance company in Philadelphia, PA, with a
single mammoth computer that occupied a large, very cold room. Dr. Thornthwaite wrote programs to run that colossal device, during the 1970s. Then,
in 1981, she began to write programs on IBM's first desktop computer. One
of those devices still sits in the back of a closet at her home.

In 1988, Dr. Thornthwaite began a decade of teaching at a large urban high school in Nashville, TN, where she was elected one year as the
school's Teacher of the Year. She taught physics, pre-engineering, and
geometry. In 1991, she was the first teacher in the school to have access
to the Internet in her classroom. The Internet was very unstable then.
When typing an e-mail, going back to correct errors was not possible. The
sender had to merely add a comment, "Oops, please ignore the error." By
the time Dr. Thornthwaite left the school for the position at Lipscomb, her

classroom contained eight computers that had been used with a variety of software programs.

At the university, Dr. Thornthwaite was responsible for running the department's computer lab. She also designed and taught most of the technology-related courses within the Department of Education. In 2006–2007, she did a great deal of research to support the beginning of an Instructional Technology M.Ed. program. That program is now provided fully online and "is designed to enhance the classroom experience by using innovative approaches to technology" (2013 Graduate Catalogue). Currently Dr. Thornthwaite teaches solely within the M.Ed. program, almost exclusively through online courses.

Dr. Thornthwaite's published works have been in the areas of technology, cultural diversity, and university-school partnerships. She has provided presentations for a variety of technology topics to dozens of local, national, and international conferences. In addition, she has provided both single and multiple day technology workshops. Recently, her workshops have focused on Web 2.0 technologies, as well as the uses of the iPad for teaching and learning in the classroom.